Praise for
Do It Right the First Time...

"I love that so many brilliant experts came together to share their wisdom in *Do It Right the First Time*. The publishing industry can be overwhelming, but this book will help writers navigate the terrain and avoid many common mistakes. Bravo!"
—Stephanie Chandler, CEO, Nonfiction Authors Association

"*Do It Right the First Time: How to Write, Publish, and Market Your Bestseller* is a powerful anthology filled with tips, tricks, and techniques from industry experts who want only the best for your publishing experience."
—Jill Lublin, 4x best-selling author, international speaker, and master publicity strategist

"We started our author journey through self-publishing, a credible way to get your words into the world. With proper guidance, you can create a professional product that enhances your brand and delivers your message to the readers you serve. Valerie J. Lewis Coleman is a knowledgeable and skilled mentor who helps writers launch the best possible print and digital products. Many writers will benefit from the guidance she generously shares."
—Mindy Kiker and Jennifer Kochert, FlourishWriters co-founders

Other books in the Do It Right Series...

Write Your Bestseller

- Writing strategies from master storytellers
- How to transfer ideas from your head to paper
- Proven resources to accelerate your success

Conversations with Marketing Experts

- Sound legal advice for copyrights, contracts, and collaborations
- The 5Cs of generating six figures from your book
- Strategies to leverage your expertise with Amazon, podcasts, and the media

Do It Right the First Time Workbook

With the volume of information shared in the three-book series, readers requested a workbook to capture aha moments, amazing discoveries, and action items. This spiral-bound book has questions, quotes, and quill space for you to move forward with your book projects. DoItTheFirstTime.com

For Kindle eBooks, visit https://amzn.to/3zeQ51j.

Do It Right the First Time: Publish, and Market Your Bestseller

Compiled by

Valerie J. Lewis Coleman

Published by
Pen of the Writer
PenOfTheWriter.com
Englewood, OH

Published by

Pen of the Writer
Englewood, OH
PenOfTheWriter.com

Copyright © 2022 by Valerie J. Lewis Coleman

All rights reserved. No part of this book may be reproduced or transmitted in any form or by any means, electronic or mechanical, without prior written consent of the publisher, except for the inclusion of brief quotes in a review.

Library of Congress Control Number: 2022914309

ISBN-13: 979-8-9865108-1-1

Edited by Valerie J. Lewis Coleman of PenOfTheWriter.com and Sharahnne Gibbons of SomethingInComma.com

Printed in the United States of America

Table of Contents

Introduction 7

Publish Your Bestseller 9
   The Tale of Two Publishers 11
     Necci Headen Cooper

   Timing Concerns…What's Realistic? 23
     Bonita M. Sparks Adams

   Designing Books that Captivate Your Readers 33
     Lisa Von De Linde

   When Self-Copyright Goes WRONG 45
     Lynita Mitchell-Blackwell, Esq.

Market Your Bestseller 53
   How to Develop YourBook Marketing Plan 55
     Susan U. Neal

   Maximizing and MonetizingBook Events 69
     Valerie J. Lewis Coleman

   Six Sensible Strategies for Selling Success 79
     Garrett M. Carter, Ph.D.

   Skyrocket Your Social Media Engagement with Nine Simple Strategies! 87
     Queashar L. Halliburton

   Don't Reinvent the Wheel, Repurpose Your Content 99
     Monique A. Chandler

Seven Tips to Speak to Sell!.. 105
   Andrea Foy

*Generating Multiple Streams of Income
from Your Book*... 115
   Denise M. Walker

Building Brand, Bridges, and Book Sales................... 121
   Noni Banks

*How I Sold Over 100,000 Copies of My Children's
Book...and Ways You Can Do It, Too!* 131
   Joylynn M. Ross

Celebrate Your Success... 139
   Valerie J. Lewis Coleman

Your Bestseller Resources....................................... 141

Introduction

I am excited to serve you on your publishing journey with advice from over thirty experts. Combined, we have hundreds of years of industry experience to help you master self-publishing to make money. We want you to succeed.

For your convenience, this series is divided into the three major aspects of publishing: writing, publishing, and marketing. No matter where you are in the process, you will gain information, insight, and inspiration to accelerate your progress.

To further catapult your success, consolidate your notes, and capture your action items, the *Do It Right the First Time Workbook* complements the series with questions, quotes, and quilling space to capture the nuggets you plan to implement. Get your copy at DoItTheFirstTime.com.

May your fingers dance across the keyboard and your pen glide across the paper as the world makes room for your gift.

Valerie J. Lewis Coleman

Valerie J. Lewis Coleman

Publish Your Bestseller

"A professional writer is an amateur who didn't quit."
—Richard Bach

Valerie J. Lewis Coleman

Do It Right the First Time
The Tale of Two Publishers

Necci Headen Cooper

The thought of being a published author was never on my to-do list. I had another plan, and so did God. The desire of publishing a book came from heaven, birthed out of a renewed path of seeking His will, finding purpose, and living to please Him. The decision to pen and publish for me came with fear, excitement, and more fear. Stepping out into an unfamiliar literary ocean will have you swimming with the fish or never leaving the shore. You are an aspiring author with the ability to transform lives. Leave the shore.

The sojourn for me started around 2004. I had to move past every negative emotion—stumbling blocks—that hindered me from publishing. Guess what happened. Overthinking reared its ugly head with self-doubt. I asked myself: "Who will buy your book? Who will read it?" These are real concerns that can be paralyzing and detrimental to the process. If you find yourself overthinking, breathe deeply. With over eight billion people on this planet, you will find your audience. Besides, your book is not about you. It is about your readers. Once you jump off the dock, envision your book in someone's hand. Seeing is believing.

To fully grasp this concept, I bought a presentation binder and created a prototype book entitled *Whispers from Heaven*. This antiquated method helped me to see greater possibilities, which became my first book. Vision takes on a life of its own. The imagination is powerful...if you use it.

After years of writing material, I wanted to be serious about moving forward. I had to think like an author and businessperson, and I had no idea what that looked like. Developing a business mindset is important for success in the literary arena. Self-publishing is a door opener to countless opportunities. One of the many benefits is that you decide your creative destiny. You may choose to produce your book independently by hiring the editors, graphic designer, formatter, printer, purchasing the International Standard Book Number (ISBN), applying for the copyright, finding literary platforms, etc. You may want to hire a professional publishing company to assist with the entire project. I chose the latter.

A word of caution: If you prefer to self-publish with a company, know that numerous scam artists are out there, waiting to steal your money. These vanity presses prey heavily on unsuspecting new authors who are desperate to get published.

It Takes Two

Two published titles. Two different publishers. Two different author names. Two different subjects, eleven years apart. Why the eleven-year gap? The short answer is the time-stealer, procrastination. Watch out for him and his lazy nephew, excuses.

Two different experiences. Both teaching moments. During my eleven-year publishing hiatus, I gained valuable information and knowledge. It took 4,015 days to get published again, and I want to help prevent this delay from happening to you.

The first time around, I did not share company with other writers, authors, or literary creatives. Being absent from social media meant I had no connections to literary experts or writers' communities. I flew solo without knowing how to fly. There was lots of trial and error, mostly error. Going solo is not a recommended publishing strategy. Communication, support, information, and accountability from other literary brilliance is crucial to the publishing process long before one book goes to print. Being disconnected will make efforts more difficult. Firsthand experience is priceless. Without community, long-term success is practically non-existent.

Google became my trusted companion to research the pros and cons of self-publishing. It is still not a substitute for real-life interactions with literary experts. It is better to ask someone in the industry than to have a search engine return a million results. Going into literary spaces helps you avoid mistakes, saving precious time and headache. After sifting through tons of information, I realized submitting a manuscript through a critically acclaimed traditional publishing house without a literary agent was impossible. The process is longer, and the author is not in full control. The appeal of self-publishing increased as a viable option.

You need to consider numerous elements to publishing. Understanding what it entails helps you calculate your strategy. You must count the cost. In self-publishing, advances or glamorous perks are not given to authors. You fully fund the project with the understanding that publishing the book is more than publishing the book. A realistic approach involves creating a workable strategy and tallying all expenses. Beyond book production, other costs include book inventory, shipping, website development, marketing, professional photos, and miscellaneous supplies. Do not let cost discourage your dream. Simply plan and execute when ready.

The Book in Review

With the first book written, I needed a publisher. Every publisher I researched used different guidelines for manuscript submissions. Although there were similarities with industry standards, some book producers (companies you hire to publish your book) offered more than others. You can contract with genre-specific companies; however, many book producers offer a wide range of services regardless of genre. I was looking for a Christian self-publisher. After an exhaustive search, I chose Xulon Press, a well-established Christian publishing house.

The way most book-producer models work is the author selects the package, submits payment, follows submission guidelines, and emails the manuscript for review and editing. Some offer editing and marketing as a la carte services. Some require an annual fee to keep books active in the company's database. Get a written contract and have an attorney review it before signing. The contract must detail the terms to protect your interests. I do not recall signing a contract with Xulon, but I recall getting a receipt for payment. Although Xulon honored the agreement, too much is at risk not to have a signed contract.

Xulon provided a short questionnaire, asking for cover ideas to forward to their graphic designer. Your cover is an invitation to check out your book. It can make or break book sales. Choose images related to the book's theme to attract potential readers. If it is unattractive, boring, or sends mixed messages, chances are it will remain in literary purgatory. The saying, "Never judge a book by its cover," has little merit. Readers do judge books by covers, titles, and content.

Once I approved the cover, the manuscript was sent to the typesetter. This stage is critical because if your manuscript has errors requiring changes, it costs extra. I had to make corrections, so I know firsthand. To avoid change fees, hire a professional editor before submitting your manuscript. Do not rely on the publisher's in-house editing.

Book pricing is important, but I didn't know anything about it…initially. I recommend researching the topic to ensure overpricing or underpricing does not occur. Page count, book format, and several other factors are used to determine retail price. Analyze titles in the same genre as your books. This useful gauge is great for studying cover designs, retail price, and more. If you select a thorough book producer, they will apply industry standards to determine the best retail price for your book. If your sole focus is recouping up-front costs or making a fast profit, exercise patience. Overpricing your book will turn off potential readers, and underpricing will leave you frustrated.

Some retailers will not accept books without a barcode. Make sure the price is embedded in the barcode and printed on the back cover. I missed this critical step with my first book. I did not know that having a price on the book added more credibility. If you want to sell the book lower than the retail price, you can. But never sell the book for more than the printed retail price. Pricing integrity is real.

In the amateur stage of my journey, I did not have an author bio, professional editor, or call-to-action statement. These basic components are essentials that should be in your book. Without a genuine collaboration with my first publisher, I did not know, and Xulon did not provide advice or suggestions. They provided an author representative to assist with minor concerns and take book orders. Whether you hire a company or publish independently, collaborate for a clear understanding of expectations. Call or email the publisher and ask questions to determine if they are suitable for you.

For my first book, Xulon created the cover design, submitted the copyright, provided the ISBN, and placed the book in their library and other outlets. They did not take royalties, a percentage of the retail price for each book sold. Like traditional publishers, some book producers take royalty payments. You should know the publisher's royalty payout system and percentage kept, if applicable. Your profit occurs after book expenses (printing, distributions costs, etc.) are paid, and whether they take royalties. Read your contract carefully. Royalties should be stated in the agreement.

Hiring a professional editor is a huge step that is often missed by new authors. I was one of them. No matter how engaging and great your content may be, potential readers can be unforgiving when it comes to grammatical errors. And like the elephant, they never forget. Avid readers set a high bar and know when books are homemade. If your goal is to write future books, an excellent writing reputation is paramount. Editing is one of the most expensive parts in self-publishing (excluding book inventory), but it's worth its weight in gold. A well-published book represents your professionalism as an author. It might be a nice gesture to ask your former English teacher to edit for you; however, if they are not skilled in professional editing, leave them to correct class papers. You are selling a body of work, which calls for a high-quality product.

Get familiar with publishing terms to remove some of the guesswork. The more knowledgeable you are, the easier it is to navigate. When choosing a publisher, be sure to investigate the publisher's website, reviews, and testimonials. When possible, get recommendations. Track your progress and keep records.

My process to publish the first book took three-and-a-half months. Publishing timelines vary from thirty days to thirty months. On February 25, 2010, *My Heart's the Pen of a Ready Writer* was released, formally introducing me into the publishing ecosystem.

Publishing is Sweeter the Second Time Around

Experience taught me that going solo for the publishing process was off the table. Entering the literary world brought a new community of authors, writers, and publishers with whom to connect.

Several years back, I attended The Red Ink Conference for aspiring writers. The impeccable line-up of speakers included some of the industry's top experts from across the nation. I was so excited to attend my first literary event. If your spending budget permits you to go to conferences, this game changer adds another layer of resources and knowledge to your investment. Participating in conferences, attending book signings, and networking changed my literary landscape. It will change yours, too.

I met my current publisher, Queen V Publishing's founder, Valerie J. Lewis Coleman, who was a speaker at the conference. While on break, we had an informative conversation. She offered a conference package about how to self-publish, which included a free thirty-minute consultation. My session with her was life changing.

Initially, I was focused on marketing and relaunching the first book. I was unable to secure my original files from Xulon, so I put the relaunch on hold. Since I had to start over, opting to publish a new book made better sense.

Although I was leaning toward QueenVPublishing.com, I researched other companies to compare services. Queen V Publishing (QVP) offered the most value. The contract was signed, and a new hassle-free publishing process began.

A meeting was scheduled to discuss the entire process in detail. We talked extensively about my goals and outcomes. I used a pen name originally. Valerie explained that it is harder to market my work with a pen name. So, I dropped it. Right after the conversation, an email was sent outlining our discussion, including extensive notes and a link to a client questionnaire. My publisher used the information to create a blueprint of exactly what I wanted. Downloadable handouts were provided, detailing everything step-by-step. I had unlimited access to ask questions. Per Valerie's recommendation, I assembled a POWER (**P**en **O**f the **W**rit**ER**) Team to critique my work, review cover options, and hold me accountable. The manuscript was professionally edited, and my author bio was crafted. We discussed titles, subtitles, and cover images. The biggest bonus: marketing training! Total collaboration was in full effect. This level of care was not offered the first time. I urge you to select the appropriate publisher to meet your needs.

My Prayer Is: Whispers and Wisdoms for the Heart released March 1, 2021. It outranked the first book in every category: quality, sales, and customer response. It debuted as a bestseller because it sold more copies through online distributors in the first month than any other QVP title! Readers post about how the book offers daily encouragements.

The negative stigma attached to poorly produced self-published titles is fading. Self-publishing is easier with many options. Online bookstores make it possible for authors to sell thousands of books without a tangible shelf. Self-publishing is not a one-author-fits-all process. Whether you choose do-it-yourself independent publishing, or you hire a book producer, understand the process. If you are engaging, interesting, and a good storyteller, publishing a quality book, along with solid marketing, results in sales. You will sell.

The more you know about publishing, the more comfortable you will be. Be teachable, persistent, and courageous, and you will go a long way. Aspiring author, you are going to be amazing! This book is a great tool, full of insight and experiences. Use it as your community of literary experts. No one should take this journey alone, especially when these contributors are waiting to share resources, tips, and recommendations to help you do it right the first time.

While many place hope in material things, Necci Headen Cooper masters trusting and hoping in the Father. Her innate passion for prayer, coupled with the desire to empower and encourage others, illuminates, radiates, and permeates. Whether released onto the pages of a book or spoken to audiences of thousands, she understands that prayer is essential to every believer. Using prayers, praise, and prose, she strives to craft a body of work that inspires you to pursue your God-given purpose. In her debut book, *My Heart's the Pen of the Ready Writer*, Necci penned words of gentleness and power reflective of God's heart. In her sophomore project, *My Prayer Is: Whispers and Wisdoms of the Heart*, she turned social media posts into epistles of thought-provoking, life-changing prayers. Her creative ingenuity has been commissioned to craft one-of-a-kind works for politicians, pastors, and personal inspiration.

Connect with Necci
NecciHeadenCooper.com
Facebook.com/NecciLand
Twitter.com/NecciHeadenCooper
Instagram.com/necci_headen_cooper

Necci's Favorite Resource
Pen of the Writer. It offers a wide range of benefits to all levels of writers seeking to leverage their craft with skill improvement, marketing, and strategies to become bestsellers. PenOfTheWriter.com

Valerie J. Lewis Coleman

Timing Concerns... What's Realistic?

Bonita M. Sparks Adams

You have to overcome many hurdles in publishing. However, I wish I had a better understanding of timing when publishing my first book. I was so happy and excited about finishing a book that I wanted it published, in my hands, and in stores a couple weeks later. I quickly found out that it doesn't happen like that. It was going to take time, and I had no idea how long it might take. I had three hurdles to overcome in reference to timing.

Timing Hurdle #1: It's Not Too Late

The first book I wrote was downloaded into me five years prior when I was asked to speak at a prayer conference. I had thirty minutes to speak on being a "secret agent" for the Lord. While preparing, the Lord downloaded information in me, and I wrote it.

I said to Him, "This is too much information to give in thirty minutes."

He said, "It is to be a book."

This event was October 31, 2015. I was so excited and felt like I wanted to publish *ACTIVATE: Secret Agents in Spiritual Warfare* by the end of the year for a launch by January 1, 2016. The problem: I had no idea how to make it happen.

I searched online and found so much information on publishing a book. I was overwhelmed! Not to mention, I didn't have the money to pay someone else to publish it for me. Then something amazing happened! In an Issachar Prophetic & Apostolic Institute Class, my instructor, Dr. Carol Sherman, told me that I could do it myself through CreateSpace. As I looked into it, it seemed like an answer to my prayers! However, I allowed the cares of life, demands of a busy schedule, finances, and waiting on help from others stop me from moving forward. I missed my deadline of January 1, 2016, and I beat myself up about it. I tend to be hard on myself.

Years later, I took a class from Tenita Johnson, which ignited my passion to write another book. I started working on it. CreateSpace no longer existed. Since it had been a few years, I felt like my consequence for not moving on the book sooner was more obstacles. I felt like the time had passed for my first book. It was outdated. There was a time and season for this book to be released, and I missed it. I had let God down because I wasn't obedient when He first encouraged me to move. Guilt brought determination. I would not be inactive with my second book, *Overwhelmed?* However, I felt God still wanted me to publish *ACTIVATE*.

My time had not passed! I found out I could publish on Kindle Direct Publishing (KDP). When God puts a passion in you to write or do something, He designates the time and season for it to come forth. Let Him guide you to accomplish the task.

Don't let the enemy (devil), others, or yourself tell you that it's too late. It is not too late! Move forward with your idea, no matter how long it has been.

Timing Hurdle #2: The Process Takes Time

The class I took from Tenita Johnson was *How to Write a 30-Day Devotional in 48 Hours*. I was so excited and wrote it in record time! I wanted the finished book in hand a month later; however, there is more to publishing than writing. Many things need to be done after the book is written including professional editing and interior formatting. I had never formatted a book, so I researched to learn how to do it. I had to have my logo and book cover designed. I needed professional photos for the cover. I created a publishing business. This all took longer than I expected.

Tenita suggested setting a goal to have something done by the end of September, thirty days after the class. Knowing my life, I gave myself some slack. I set goals for the end of October, November, and December for *Overwhelmed? Finding Help in Psalm 37 Devotional & Journal*. My book-in-hand goal was the beginning of 2019. I did all of this while working as a high school business teacher, writing and producing plays, being active in my church, helping my husband with other businesses, and fulfilling roles as wife, mother, grandmother, and daughter. I stressed myself trying to make these self-imposed deadlines. I encouraged myself through my book because I was feeling overwhelmed! I had to learn how to upload a book to Amazon and IngramSpark. Time passed waiting for the proof copy, making corrections, and reprinting. I missed my deadline…again.

Looking back on the situation, I realize that I had unrealistic expectations. I learned as I went and didn't know how much time would be involved in each step. The only rush to get things done was me pushing myself. Had I known what to expect, I could have created a realistic timeframe, and saved myself lots of anxiety. Once I learned the process, I published the next book in record time! However, when I was ready to publish my first children's book, I had another learning curve. I had no idea how long getting illustrations can take! My lesson learned: each step takes time. It is best to do things right the first time. Do not give in to the temptation of accepting less-than-perfect in an effort to be done. It's best to be patient through this process.

Timing Hurdle #3: The Best Time to Release My Book

I researched on Google, attended webinars and classes, and networked to figure out how to get my book published. I took classes from Valerie J. Lewis Coleman. I wanted her or Tenita to publish my book; however, I felt very strongly that the Lord wanted me to do it myself. I needed to know how to publish and then use my knowledge to help others. Determined to not let another year pass without my books being published, I set a new goal of January 1, 2020.

I am so thankful to my launch team. Tamika Adams-Sajdak, Rev. Vernice Muldrew, Apostle Shelia Sudberry, Yolanda Ferguson, and Shari Thompson encouraged me. They reminded me to stop being hard on myself. I am thankful to my mom, Rev. Shirley A. Sparks, and my best friend, Dr. Karen Adams-Ferguson, because they prayed me through. And my dear husband, James, was supportive. I am grateful that he put up with me spending hours at the computer instead of with him.

I missed the January 1 deadline. I refocused my efforts for a March release of both books. I wanted to debut the timing of my books with Women's History Month, my birthday, and wedding anniversary. I did everything I knew to do to hit the mark, then COVID-19 hit. What a letdown. I accepted that postponing the launch was best due to quarantine. I set Easter as the new release date. Another letdown. Surely, I could launch by Mother's Day and dedicate the books to my mother. Yet another disappointment. I threw up my hands and said, "Lord, You had me write these books. I'm going to trust that when You want them released, they will be released."

June 18, 2020, *ACTIVATE: Secret Agents in Spiritual Warfare* and *Overwhelmed? Finding Help in Psalm 37 Devotional & Journal* were released on Amazon. I can't explain the joy I felt. Although I missed previous dates that had special significance, I didn't care. I was happy that I had published not one, but two books! Shari, a member on my launch team, called to congratulate me.

"This is so awesome. You released your books on Juneteenth!"

I didn't realize it.

The Holy Spirit said, "Just like Juneteenth was the day slaves found out they were free, even though they had been freed already, people who read your books will be set free."

I was so happy that God had honored my request and allowed my books to release on a day that had significance. Although I tried to release the books earlier in the year, God's timing was perfect. I hosted a drive-by book signing. People were comfortable staying in their cars to support me. It was not too late, but right on time!

Having learned the publishing process, I get things done much faster. However, when you use others for services like editing, cover design, formatting, and illustrations, it can take more time. Delays happen. Don't get discouraged when things don't happen when you think they should. As a person of faith and prayer, I believe things occur at set times. If you pray and trust the Lord, He allows things to occur when they are supposed to happen. Following the Lord's leading, I was able to self-publish four books in less than one year! Moving in God's timing makes all the difference.

General Timeframe for Publishing a Book

How long does it take to publish a book? What is a realistic timeframe? Self-publishing is usually faster than traditional publishing. For a first-time publisher, it could take a couple months for a short eBook and up to twelve months or more for a print book. The timeframe varies depending on several factors:

- How well the manuscript is written and word count determine how much editing is needed.
- How quickly you learn to do tasks.
- How long it takes to find, interview, and hire professionals for delegated tasks.

Be sure to factor in unexpected delays. You will shrink the time to publication once you learn the process.

This table provides a general timeframe for publishing:

Activity	Weeks
Developmental editing involves rewording, rewriting, and restructuring.	2-8
Copy editing searches for word usage, facts, and consistency.	1-4
Proofreading for spelling and grammatical errors.	1-4
Copyright and Library of Congress Control Number (LCCN) filing	1-2
Interior formatting and layout for printing	1-5
eBook formatting	1-4
Cover design depends on the designer's experience, complexity, and your satisfaction with the results.	1-5
Illustrations depend on the illustrator's expertise, style, number and complexity of illustrations, and how quickly you are happy with the results.	1-12
Waiting for print proof copy. Note: If you find an error in the proof, you have to correct, resubmit, and wait for another proof.	1-2
Book printing depends on book format (paperback, hardcover, spiral-bound), printer's in-house functions, turn-around time, and shipping method.	2-6
Total	12-52

Bonita M. Sparks Adams is the CEO of Write The Vision Publishing, LLC. This author, award-winning playwright, and coach is also an accomplished teacher, producer, and speaker. She uses her self-publishing lessons learned to help others "get it done" in an affordable manner. Bonita is a vessel who "delivers" people from what holds them back. Her inspirational self-help books and journals make the challenges of daily life easier to manage.

Connect with Bonita
WriteTheVisionPub.com
Amazon.com/author/bonitamsparksadams
Facebook.com/bonitasparksadams
Linkedin.com/in/bonitasparksadams

Bonita's Favorite Resource
Google Search Engine

Valerie J. Lewis Coleman

Do It Right the First Time

Designing Books that Captivate Your Readers

Lisa Von De Linde

In getting it right the first time, it is essential to hire an experienced book cover designer. What it takes to design a book cover is different from the graphic design skills required for platforms like websites, social media, or online/print advertising.

The details matter when you want your self-published book to be on par with books by traditional publishing houses. The old adage, "Don't judge a book by its cover" isn't exactly true. While it is good advice to refrain from judging based on appearances only, people *do* judge books by their covers. Cover design *does* matter. An untrained eye can spot a poorly designed book, even if it's only a subconscious awareness.

Many factors cause bad cover design as noted in the partial list below:
- Wrong font sizes
- Too many fonts
- Unreadable fonts
- Imagery that does not engage your audience
- Colors that don't align with your topic or audience
- Bad layout
- Incorrect spine width

- Elements missing on the spine
- Barcode formatting
- Back cover design that does not meet industry standards

As a self-published author, investing in book design is one step you can take to help your book succeed. Working with a skilled book designer leaves a great first—and lasting—impression. Whether grabbing the book off a shelf or spotting the cover amidst a sea of online search results, a well-designed cover can create enough interest for someone to read the synopsis.

TIP: Walk through a bookstore or library and pick up books in your genre. Pay attention to the front, spine, and back cover design details. Based on the quality, guess if the book is from a traditional publishing house or a self-published author (the copyright page may provide the answer). Use this information to balance personal preferences with traditional publishing standards and trust your book designer's expertise.

Choosing a Book Designer

Most self-published authors release a printed book with other formats as add-ons. Designing printed books requires a specialized skill set that is becoming rarer to find. Quality book design involves intricate, specialized expertise. You want the designer you hire to create books to the same standard as traditional publishing houses.

Key things to request before hiring a designer:
- Examples of print design projects, which require a different skill set than designs for digital/online purposes
- Portfolio examples that include published books versus unpublished pre-made or mockup covers
- Genres of books they design. As with editors and illustrators, not all designers are a good match for your book.

It's not a good idea to save money by hiring a designer who has no experience with book publishing, especially if you want to do it right the first time. Poor design can negatively affect your book sales and tarnish your brand. Investing in an established expert saves money in the long run as you avoid the cost for redesign and the frustration of lost sales.

Print is more permanent than social media or a website, which can be easily changed. Once your book is printed (and your eBook/audiobook files uploaded), making changes requires publishing a new edition. It's important to do it right the first time so you don't have a massive inventory of unsaleable books. Working with a book design expert gives you peace of mind.

TIP: Ask your designer about other book-related services they provide—landing pages, 3D book mockups, print/digital marketing materials, social media graphics, and physical products (bookmarks, postcards, journals, workbooks, and event signage) to sell or use at events. Having the same designer gives a cohesive look to everything connected to your book. If your book designer does not provide other design services, request a font and color list for the graphic designer you hire to create marketing material.

The Design Process

Book design is a custom service. Your book is unique in content, audience, and length. A 1,000-word children's book has vastly different page count, pricing, and completion timeline compared to a 100,000-word novel. Manuscripts vary from plain text (fiction or memoirs) to features like lists, pull quotes, tables, charts, photographs, and illustrations. The more complex the manuscript, the more intensive the time and design work.

It is helpful to have a rough draft of your manuscript when contacting designers to provide an estimated word count. Other essentials are title, subtitle, book dimensions, publishing formats, book category, and international standard book number (ISBN). Be prepared to discuss these details with your designer for answers to your questions and guidance to helpful resources.

Once you've hired a designer, you will discuss your ideas and inspiration related to the design elements—fonts, colors, images, and layout. It's ideal to share what you do and don't like in the beginning including book covers, font styles, colors, and any guidance based on your branding. Your designer will use your inspiration to develop ideas for the design direction. For my design process, I send clients a detailed questionnaire to gather essential information before design work begins.

TIP: Format options for books are paperback, hard cover, hard cover with dustjacket, eBook, and audiobook. With the ease of print-on-demand services, I recommend publishing the print version *and* an eBook. Since designing a print interior is the first step in creating an eBook, publishing *only* an eBook does not save time or design services.

Timeline and Investment

Four months is a good baseline to allow for the cover and interior design process. This ensures enough time to avoid rushing or missing deadlines with printers or launch plans. Some books, especially those with custom illustrations or extensive features like a glossary or index, take longer.

Design timeframes do not include printing and shipping. When an author wants printed copies for launch events, I advise adding at least one month in their marketing/launch schedule. Check production lead times with the printer. If you work with a local printer, ship time is minimal. If your printer is on the other side of the world, plan accordingly.

High-end book design starts in the thousands. Yes, you can spend less; however, you don't want to cut corners on quality to save a few dollars. Investing in design helps you succeed.

TIP: Concept development for high-end book cover design doesn't happen on demand. Don't rush the creative process. Remember, the goal is to craft the best solution for your book's first impression.

Front Cover

The front cover is the first step of designing a book. Some covers require an intensive concept development and image research. Many hours of brainstorming, sketching, and searching royalty-free stock-art websites are required. Custom artwork for the cover or interior (i.e., photoshoot or illustrations) typically involves a third party, adding time and money to the creative process.

Front cover design checklist:
- Keep the words readable in font style and size.
- Use one contrasting font for the subtitle and author name.
- Put the author's name at the bottom edge.
- Don't use a photo of yourself on the cover.

Whether your book is designed to be on-brand or stand on its own is a decision to discuss with your designer. When it aligns with your publishing goals, keeping the design on-brand can be achieved through color choices, even if fonts and images are distinct from your branding.

TIP: Don't do a general online search for images or artwork except as inspiration for your designer. Most photographs and illustrations require the purchase of a license for the right to use them. It is best to find them on stock or royalty-free sites to ensure you obtain the proper license. Your designer can recommend websites for images to match your cover concept. See *Intellectual Property for Authors* by Nakia Gray, Esq. in *Do It Right the First Time: Conversations with Marketing Experts*.

After the front cover is approved, the interior design and layout phase begins. This part of the process is referred to as typesetting or formatting.

Page Design

The first step of interior formatting starts with page design to determine the overall look of your interior including margins, line spacing, fonts, chapter titles, page numbers, and any features in the manuscript.

Many details affect the readability of your book: kerning, leading, tracking, rivers of white, bleed, gutters, orphans, widows, and white space. Your book expert will know these terms and how they affect your book layout. When these aspects are not designed based on publishing standards, your book's readability is hampered. Readers may have no idea what caused their reaction to a badly designed book. They just know they didn't like the experience of reading it. If they don't finish your book or struggle to read it, you will lose readers, referrals, and reviews.

Typesetting

After the page design sample is approved, the next step is typesetting. Your designer creates the full interior layout, line-by-line, checking details to make sure every paragraph and page are set for maximum readability.

TIP: After formatting is complete, hire a professional proofreader to review page layouts along with grammar and spelling mistakes. These typos and minor textual changes must be made before giving final approval for the interior.

Spine and Back Cover

After the interior is approved, the page count is finalized, and the last phase of cover design happens. Page count, binding, and type of paper are needed to determine the width of your book's spine. Using those specs and the book's trim size, your print platform may prepare a correctly sized cover template. Then, the spine and back cover can be designed.

Book spines need the title, author's name, and publisher logo (if you have one). In the case of a long title, sometimes only the author's last name is used on the spine. If your book is part of a series, it is good to include design elements on the spine indicating the series and order.

Back cover design checklist:
- Headline-attention grabbing catchphrase or probing question
- Description—marketing copy designed to help readers connect with your message
- Endorsements and reviews
- Professional author photo (no more than 1.5" x 1.5")
- Author bio that's two to three sentences
- Logo and website
- ISBN and barcode with the retail price embedded
- Retail price
- Book category (BISAC code)

The back cover is the next key place to capture your audience's interest. Design *and* content matter. Write strategically so readers want more. Breaking up the text with a headline phrase and two or three short paragraphs (include a bulleted list if appropriate), make for an interesting layout and is easier to read.

TIP: Select an appropriate category to provide booksellers and libraries a guide for where to place your book. Book Industry Standards and Communications (BISAC) creates an industry-approved list of subject descriptors consisting of nine-character alphanumeric codes. The latest edition of the BISAC Subject Heading list is available at BISG.org. The category code is positioned near the barcode.

Final Files

After final approval is given for the cover and interior, printer-ready files are prepared for publishing. Typically, you receive press-ready PDFs of the interior and complete cover — front, spine, and back. Your designer keeps the source or native-layered files (i.e., Adobe InDesign) for revisions and future editions.

Other Formats

After the interior is approved, eBook conversion and audiobook recording can happen. You don't want to start these formats before the print version is final as proofreading may incur manuscript changes. Adjustments to the layout may be needed to create a better reader/listener experience in each add-on format. A uniquely sized front-cover image must be prepared for digital display of each format. Standards vary by platform.

TIP: eBooks are reflowable because readers can adjust font, size, and color on their devices. Some aspects of the print design may not translate perfectly to the reflowable nature of eBooks. To address this matter, notify your designer of your intentions to publish an eBook at the start of the design process.

Pitfalls to Avoid
Licensing

Fonts, photographs, and artwork require licenses for usage rights. When you take your professional author photos, or invest in a photoshoot with models, you must have releases signed by people who appear in the photos. The releases should indicate current and future uses to prevent litigation. Be aware of the backgrounds in your photos. To avoid infringing on someone's intellectual property, only artwork that is your original creation should appear in photos. See *Intellectual Property for Authors* by Nakia Gray, Esq. in *Do It Right the First Time: Conversations with Marketing Experts*.

TIP: Review the license terms for your cover artwork as some licenses have a usage restriction. Selling a massive number of books may require you to publish a new edition or update the license. Congratulations! Selling tons of books is a good problem.

Subtitle

Your title and subtitle should be finalized before cover design begins. However, it may be necessary to reword your subtitle for more cohesiveness with the desired imagery. When done correctly, rephrasing can improve the overall appeal of your cover.

TIP: Discuss cover wording changes with your book designer. A significant shift in wording—longer/shorter or more/fewer—may require a redesign, costing you time and money.

Process

Cover design and interior design do not have to be performed by the same designer; however, the process flows smoother when you hire one expert to do both. The inherent dilemma with hiring two designers is delays due to miscommunication and design issues. Working with one designer eliminates this concern.

TIP: Be flexible with your publishing timeline so you can hire the designer who will do your book right the first time. Since people judge books by their covers, investing in a designer with publishing experience will help your book succeed.

While book design may seem daunting, partnering with the right expert will make a world of difference during the process and for the quality of your published book.

Lisa is a graphic designer and owner of LisaVdesigns, an Ohio-based studio that partners with authors, entrepreneurs, and organizations. She provides custom design services for all things related to book publishing and brand identity systems. Since 2004, she has designed books for traditional publishing houses and self-published authors. She is passionate about partnering with purpose-driven businesses, especially those championing a cause. Lisa brings your vision to life through strategic project planning and creative design services that give you that I'm-an-expert edge.

Connect with Lisa
LisaVDesigns.com
Facebook.com/LisaVdesigns
Linkedin.com/in/lisavondelinde
Instagram.com/lisavdesigner

Lisa's Favorite Resource
MyIdentifiers.com to learn about and purchase ISBNs for book publishing.

Do It Right the First Time

When Self-Copyright Goes WRONG

Lynita Mitchell-Blackwell, Esq.

"Lynita, someone has taken my title and my book art! I want to sue her for violating my copyright, but I can't find my copyright registration. Has it been completed?"

Those words are the last ones you want to hear as a publisher. And they're even worse to say as a writer. Yet that happened with one of my authors years ago. How, you ask? By not following The Publishers Blueprint.

At all times, your work is your work. Just as you protect anything else that belongs to you, your written words must be protected as well. But the protection does not begin with copyright; it begins in your mind and then your actions. Your mind and actions must be aligned, and they must follow a process, a system, a BLUEPRINT.

When I used to publish authors, I had the benefit of going through it myself. I self-published my own books, so I knew about writing, revision, editing, proofreading, formatting, cover design, photoshoots, publishing, copywriting, printing, selling, and marketing. It is lots of work, and it is very easy to lose yourself in the process. That is why I created a project flow process in a project management system to ensure nothing fell through the cracks.

In developing that system for myself, I had a tried-and-true roadmap to use for my clients. And it worked...until I had "that one." The one where I did not follow the road map because I had genuine compassion for the author's situation.

Before I go into "the situation," a word of caution: compassion and empathy are blessings. These qualities make you a better person, a phenomenal writer, and an award-winning visionary. But without a clear path as to how you plan to help a person, your feelings can compromise your objectivity and lead you to circumvent the very processes you put in place to ensure you stay organized and professional. Okay, now back to "the situation."

This author and I did not do anything in order. We started, and then her father died. She grieved for several months (understandably!) and got back on track. She worked a few months, and then her mother died. This time, grief took down this author. She set aside the project for a couple of years.

One day, I had a feeling, more like a whisper really, to go forward and get that author's book out into the world. I was excited and felt good about pursuing the inclination. The author felt good and pushed forward as well. But in following that feeling, I did not follow the process. We checked all the boxes, getting everything done — not in order — but they got done. Her published book was well received.

And then I received the email: "I can't find my copyright!"

My heart dropped. Even though I knew that it should have been done, and I normally do it, because this author's situation was so unique, I knew that I would not find the copyright registration as I searched. And I didn't.

I almost died.

I thought about our options. Some would say that the copyright was established once the work was completed. The copyright is a protection and registration with the US government establishing that work you created is yours and originated with you. Literally, it is original work for which you want to be compensated if someone else wants to use it. It allows you to license the use of your work. Without filing the appropriate paperwork, no such license exists. Therefore, the most you could do is send a cease-and-desist letter to stop the person from using your work. You may also be able to obtain an injunction from a court to stop the use of the work, but no financial benefit will result. Neither of these options allows you to obtain financial compensation for the unauthorized use of your work.

Others will tell you that you could self-copyright your work. The first time I heard that term, believe it or not, was at a writer's conference by a very well-known publisher who is no longer in business. They published some of the hottest romance novels. They were on the cutting edge of a variety of genres that no one else would touch. They created a wonderful niche for themselves while putting a bunch of bad information about copyright procedures into the world.

Self-copyright is a term used by those who are too cheap to spend $65 to protect their work. And when I use the term cheap, I do not mean it from the perspective of don't-want-to-pay-because-they-don't-have-the-money. I use it to indicate laziness and a lack of regard for their own work's protection and integrity. And that is nonsensical. Honestly, that is crazy! Self-copyright involves sending a copy of your work via email to yourself and utilizing that date stamp to establish the origination of the work. The problem is that anybody could do that, and it does not prove anything other than the fact that the email originated with you. Most document creation products now have a date stamp showing the date that the document was created. What if someone says you emailed the document to yourself May 3, 1999, but the document was created May 3, 1997? Wouldn't it make sense for the copyright protection to originate at the time of creation?

Needless to say, it will be difficult to fight to protect your work relying on an email date.

So how do you protect your work?
1. Go to the official US copyright website Copyright.gov.
2. Complete the relatively simple application that will take you twenty minutes tops.

3. Upload an electronic copy of the work, which is recommended, or mail a physical copy to the office.
4. Pay the appropriate fee.
5. Wait for your registration letter.

It really is that simple! And if you do not want to do it yourself, have your publisher do it. That is really their job.

And speaking of jobs…whatever happened to the author for whom I did not file the copyright on time? The first thing I did was calm my author. I was honest and told her that I did not follow my process because of her extenuating circumstances. I had thrown out my blueprint. I apologized and told her that I would get right on looking at our options, which I did. Next, I obtained a copy of the book in question and reviewed it.

Although the book title was similar, it was not the same. Although the verbiage in the book was similar, it was not the same either. And the book was published a few months after my client's book. Nevertheless, the books had enough differences that my client's work was still protected. I filed an expedited copyright application that day, which was granted. My client's work, and her rights, were protected.

Every situation does not end happily as this one did. I am happy to say that my author has sold many books, became a bestseller, and is doing well with speaking engagements. But I believe that things worked out the way they did because, even though we did not follow my original process and checklist, we got back on track as soon as I realized we had a problem.

Invest in yourself, invest in your work, and invest in processes to protect yourself and your work. You will not regret it!

Lynita Mitchell-Blackwell is the Supreme Performance and personal and professional development coach. An attorney, CPA, certified Christian life coach, and new thought minister, Lynita founded several businesses, including an eponymous law firm through which she has been recognized as a Top 100 Lawyer; an award-winning media company that published five magazines, two of which were voted as ATL's Hottest; a publishing company that produced eight best-selling authors; and a leadership development non-profit. Unfortunately, with every professional "win" came a corresponding "loss." A brutal battle with endometriosis, struggles with self-esteem, and career changes that created terrifying fork-in-the-road decisions, tried to diminish her success. As a national best-selling author and transformational keynote speaker, Lynita enjoys helping others face their fears, transform their pain, and position themselves to experience the reign of blessings.

Connect with Lynita
LynitaMitchellBlackwell.com
Facebook.com/LynitaMitchellBlackwell
Linkedin.com/in/LynitaMitchellBlackwell
Instagram.com/lynitamitchellblackwellesq
Twitter.com/lynitamb

Lynita's Favorite Resource
Copyright.gov because it's the official place to file a US copyright.

Valerie J. Lewis Coleman

Market Your Bestseller

"If writing and publishing a book are like birthing a child, then book marketing is like rearing it."

—Heather Hart

Valerie J. Lewis Coleman

Do It Right the First Time

How to Develop Your Book Marketing Plan

Susan U. Neal

Writing and publishing your book is not the end of your job as an author. Now you want to get it into the hands of readers. To increase sales, you must let more people know your book exists. Whether self-published or traditionally published, you are responsible for marketing your book. Therefore, every author needs a strategic plan to successfully promote each book.

Have you thought about how you will market your book? You can use various media outlets such as blogs, magazines, podcasts, radio shows, and television. While taking on marketing yourself may be a challenge, don't let the process intimidate you. Instead, learn to create your book's strategic marketing plan. This chapter will show you how.

Book Reviews

Reviews are one of the most vital and impactful ways to promote your book. This step of marketing happens before your book is released. Prior to publication, create a book review team. Weeks before publication, I send a copy of my book via BookFunnel.com to team members and ask them to post a review within two weeks of the book's release.

I use BookFunnel because only one person can open a book link from this site. Therefore, your manuscript cannot be shared with anyone else. You can also send your team promotional memes for your book that they can share on social media channels.

Initial book reviews are vital, but you can't stop there. Continuing to request reviews is an essential component of any book's salability. Whenever I receive positive feedback from a reader, I respond by thanking them and asking them to post a review on Amazon. I send the Amazon link, so it is easy for them to click and post the review. I also ask readers who benefited from my book to post on their social media networks. It never hurts to ask. I specifically request they post a photo of them holding my book along with a brief comment on how they benefited from it.

Continue to request reviews from friends, family, and members of book clubs or writers' groups once the book has launched. When I give my book to someone, I add a reminder on my calendar to contact them in two months to request a review. It is the least they can do. Be brave and ask!

After you get fifty Amazon book reviews, more reviews post organically without solicitation. So, work hard to get those first fifty positive reviews. To learn more about obtaining book reviews, take the Christian Indie Publishing Association (CIPA) course: "Tips for Getting More Book Reviews" at CIPA.Podia.com.

Media Kit

A media kit is an excellent marketing tool. A professionally created media kit (a one-page marketing sheet or "one sheet") includes the book cover, description, bio, headshot, book reviews, media release quote, and interview questions and answers. Sending a media kit along with your new book's media release to local and regional newspapers works well. I place my media kit in Dropbox and attach the link to emails. This technique eliminates the risk of a newspaper opening a document with a virus. My local paper wrote a front-page article about my books, and a regional one ran a feature story. I also include my media kit when asking to be interviewed on a podcast.

While a media kit should be professional, you can hire an expert or learn to create one yourself. If you need help producing your media kit, download the free Author Media Kit Guide at the bottom of ChristianPublishers.net. Instead of emailing a one sheet, I created a media page at SusanUNeal.com/media and a media kit at SusanUNeal.com/press-kit. Now I send media contacts to one of these pages.

Marketing Plan

Marketing is not an occasional effort to promote your book. Authors need a strategic plan, which varies depending on the author, type of book, etc. My plan was based on several monthly goals for the first year of my book's publication: publishing a magazine article, writing a guest blog post, and being interviewed on a podcast or radio show.

I attended Christian writers' conferences where I met magazine editors and pitched different topics — based on my book — that might interest their readers. As I met other conferees, I asked them if they had a blog or podcast. If yes, I asked if I could write a guest blog or be interviewed on their podcast. Whenever someone sends me a friend request on social media, I check to see if they host a relevant blog or podcast. If yes, I reach out through the app's direct messaging and ask if they would interview me.

It is strategic to be a guest blogger on websites with a decent domain authority (search engine ranking score). If a link to my website (at the end of my guest blog) was on a website with low traffic and domain authority, that could harm my website's ranking on Google. Marketing can be tricky! To determine a website's domain authority, go to Moz.com/domain-analysis#index. Enter the website's domain name and click Analyze. Before pitching an article, make sure the website's domain authority is above twenty. Closer to fifty is better.

To begin your marketing plan, list the different web venues for which you could write a guest blog. Next, create a list of magazines for which you could write. When you are first starting out, online magazines may be best. You can find opportunities to write articles and blogs in *The Christian Writers Market Guide* and *Writers Market*. For me, the best way is personally meeting editors and conferees at conferences. Writers' conferences are also listed in these guidebooks, or you can conduct an online search. Budget conference and travel fees as you create your marketing plan.

Podcast and radio tours increase your exposure to a whole new audience without paying for advertising. Create a list of radio and podcast shows and email them your pitch. You can purchase the course: "How to Book a Podcast Tour" and "List of Over 125 Radio & Podcast Media" at CIPA.Podia.com. The media outlets are listed by genre with contact information.

Before you query, determine the show's audience size to ensure it is worth your time to be a guest. A good indication of audience size is based on the show's number of iTunes reviews. The larger the number of reviews, the larger the audience. Go to the show's iTunes listing and check for the number of ratings listed under the show's title. If the podcast has less than ten reviews, its audience size is tiny. Reviews from ten to twenty-five indicate a small size. Twenty-five to fifty denotes a moderate following, and over fifty signifies the show has a good following. At first, you will most likely need to be a guest on smaller-sized shows. Before querying, listen to the show and write a review for it on iTunes. Send the host an email with your media kit attached via Dropbox. A podcast tour is a highly effective, inexpensive means of placing books before new readers.

You won't know which marketing tactic worked best unless you track the results. So, I created a spreadsheet that lists the marketing method, number of website visits, Amazon book rank, and book sales over three days. Then, I highlighted the technique that brought the top results. By reviewing the results, I know where to focus future marketing efforts.

Social Media

Social media algorithms change regularly, so a successful tactic one year may not be effective the next. However, these platforms allow you to engage with your audience. Be aware that not just any post is effective. Information you post on social media to market your book needs to be beneficial to your target audience. Figure out how your posts can benefit your audience or ask them for their input, as people love to give their opinion. A common rule is to post once about yourself for every five posts that benefit your audience. Ask a stimulating question at the end of each post to get more engagement. When someone comments on your post, ask them a question in return. For example, "It was so nice to meet you at the writers' conference. Do you plan to attend next year?" They will likely answer your question. When a social media platform recognizes that you engage your audience, the post is shown to more of your followers. Talk with people on social media like you were speaking with them in person. The more you do, the more social media will work for you.

Use a scheduling program to post your social media. I use PostPlanner.com because it allows me to repost an item as often as I want. Hootsuite and Buffer are other social media scheduling systems. I use TailwindApp.com to post on Instagram and Pinterest. Most authors want to write, not work on social media. Still, publishers demand a platform, and using a scheduler can grow your platform. When you use a scheduling program, you decrease the time you spend on social media. In one evening, you can schedule posts for an entire month.

Unfortunately, with most social media sites, it is a pay-to-play culture. Amazon, Instagram, Facebook, and other platforms offer ads. If you purchase ads, the platform shows your post to more people. Take a course about creating ads on these platforms and try it. Amazon ads can be expensive until you get the hang of it, so pay close attention to your ads and how much you are spending. Then, evaluate their effectiveness for future ad decisions.

Bookstore Events

The best time for an in-person bookstore event is Black Friday through the first week in January because stores are busiest. A Barnes & Noble manager told me that mid-September through the end of November is another great time for in-store events. It is fun to share a book event with another author, so invite a friend from a writers' group to join you.

Contact your local and regional bookstores about hosting a book event. Set your book's floor banner next to your table and a tabletop banner displaying another one of your books, if you have one. If people are not stopping by your table, stand by the door, greet customers, and hand them your book. Explain that you are a local author autographing copies today. Let them know that they can return the book to your table if they are not interested in purchasing it.

The greatest thing about in-store events is that you develop a relationship with the bookstore owner or manager. That is key because this person decides whether to carry your book in their store. Tell the manager that you would be happy to participate in any future author events. When you spend your valuable time at their store and promote them on social media (tag the store and the manager), you become the store's ally.

Every December, I schedule bookstore events at three different Barnes & Noble stores within a ninety-minute drive from my home. The last time I stopped by the Destin Barnes & Noble, I was pleasantly surprised to find my book, *Solving the Gluten Puzzle*, displayed face out along with a sign under it, "Celiac Disease/Gluten-Free." Wow! That is marketing at its best. Visit bookstores when traveling and drop off a copy of your book along with a one sheet. Another way to get your books carried in Christian bookstores is through the Christian Product Expo (CPE) Show.

Trade Shows

Trade shows provide the perfect opportunity to find media and retail outlets. Attend the CPE and National Religious Broadcasters (NRB) conventions. The night before the CPE, fifty-plus authors display their books at the book signing party. Over a hundred Christian bookstore owners visit each author to receive a free, autographed book. The owners get a great selection of Christian books they can choose to carry in their bookstore. As an author, you can attend the CPE through the CIPA or Advanced Writers and Speaker Association (AWSA.com) and participate in the book signing party. My book sales through the IngramSpark publishing platform quadrupled after I attended my first CPE.

The NRB convention hosts over seven-hundred exhibitors and a pressroom where all forms of media interview attendees. At the convention, I was filmed for a ten-minute slot on a television show and invited to two other Christian television talk shows, with expenses paid, except airfare. You can attend this show for the least expensive price through the CIPA.

Writers' Conferences

Conferences are not just for learning about writing and the book industry or finding marketing opportunities with other conferees but also for cultivating industry relationships. During a conference, be sure to collect business cards of publishing professionals and authors. When you return home, visit everyone's website and friend them on each social media network. As they reciprocate, you begin to build a following. Continue to stay in contact with these incredible individuals.

Pitching an article to an editor face-to-face at a conference has always gotten my articles published, while a query letter has not. Before the conference, I investigate every faculty member to see if they write for or are an editor of a magazine. I make an appointment with each one at the conference. With the editors, I pitch an article or two. With the writers, I ask how they got the opportunity to write for their magazines. Be bold; it doesn't hurt to ask.

Other conferees may have blogs, podcasts, book critique sites, or perform author interviews. It is vital to meet others who are on this writing journey. You never know how a fellow conferee might boost your career or become a friend. If you meet someone who has a blog or podcast, ask if you can be a guest. Make a list of conferences you want to attend next year, and plan ahead.

Writers' conferences often sponsor book contests. Enter your published book in as many reputable contests as possible. After you win an award, send a media release to local and regional newspapers. After my book, *7 Steps to Get Off Sugar and Carbohydrates*, won the 2018 Selah Award at the Blue Ridge Mountains Christian Writers Conference, I added the contest emblem to the front cover. It sold over four hundred copies per month in the following eight months. Check out potential book contests and make a plan to enter one or more.

Author Associations

Professional associations are formed for the purpose of collaborating and learning from one another, with the idea that shared knowledge and experience provides better results than doing it alone. Information gleaned from membership in a publishing association can improve your writing, publishing, and book marketing efforts. Publishing associations also provide opportunities to network with other authors and industry professionals. Networking leads to doors opening through collaborations.

Check out the CIPA benefits at ChristianPublishers.net/membership. CIPA was created in 2004 to provide authors with resources to publish professionally and market effectively. Learning about the publishing industry is challenging. CIPA discounts, educational materials, and marketing tools make your experience easier and more profitable. Other associations to consider include AWSA, American Christian Fiction Writers Association, American Christian Writers, Christian Authors Network, and Evangelical Christian Publishers Association.

Summary

Marketing comprises a large part of an author's work. When more people know about your book, you achieve higher sales. Therefore, developing an intentional book-marketing plan is crucial. Are you doing enough to market your book? No one will promote your masterpiece as passionately as you.

I recommend writing a monthly plan that includes:
- I will submit a guest blog to _____
- I will submit an article to _____
- I will submit requests for interviews to the following podcasts or radio shows _____

After you streamline your marketing tactics, start writing your next book. Work with a professional editor to polish the first three chapters and book proposal. Then, send it to your agent for distribution or pitch it at a writers' conference. Continue to work on your previous book's marketing as you write your manuscript. You don't know which one of your books will be a bestseller, so keep writing! When you publish another book, it introduces readers to the backlist of books you previously published.

Book marketing is not for the faint of heart. You have to get out there and hustle. A writing career is like a juggling act. Every day you get on that stage and juggle the many facets of this God-given, crazy-making, fun career.

As a certified AWSA writer coach, Susan Neal RN, MBA, MHS, desires to help others publish and sell their God-given message. She is the author of eight healthy living books. Her self-published number one Amazon bestseller, *7 Steps to Get Off Sugar and Carbohydrates*, won the Selah Award and sold over 20,000 copies in four years. Susan won the 2020 Christian Author Network Crown Award for Outstanding Broadcast Media for her book marketing campaign. She is a trusted advisor for authors and helps many sell more books. Susan is the director of the Christian Indie Publishing Association (CIPA) which teaches authors how to self-publish professionally and market effectively.

Connect with Susan
SusanUNeal.com
Facebook.com/SusanUllrichNeal
LinkedIn.com/in/SusanNealYoga
Instagram.com/HealthyLivingSeries
Twitter.com/SusanNealYoga

Susan's Favorite Resource
Advanced Marketing Institute's headline analyzer. This free tool assesses the emotional value of your message considering the ratio between intellectual, emotional, and spiritual words. AMInstitute.com/headline

Valerie J. Lewis Coleman

Do It Right the First Time

Maximizing and Monetizing Book Events

Valerie J. Lewis Coleman

Most authors are right-brained introverts. The thought of having to engage with readers can be frightening and overwhelming. Having attended hundreds of book events, I witnessed authors sitting behind tables, head bowed, as potential customers walked past. Incorporating the following ideas can help improve your book sales.

Pre-event
Three to six months before the event, start promoting. Regardless of the event host's marketing campaign, individual promotion is essential to ensure that people come to the event specifically for you. Post the event on your website, Facebook, and GoodReads.com's author page. Keep in mind that social media is a great tool to invite people; however, personal invites via email, text, and phone calls are more effective. Invite book clubs and writers' groups. These audiences are avid readers who often look for book fairs, author appearances, and writing resources. LinkedIn is great to identify professionals in specific areas. If you've already made a cyber introduction, inbox them to let them know that you'll be in the area. Invite them to the event or coordinate

a meeting over coffee. Even if you're going to a new city, you don't know who you know who knows someone there. Ask your friends, family, and fans to share your appearance. Their vouching for you goes much further than a cold call.

Submit your participation to online community calendars. If you want to be included in printed newspaper calendars, submit your information at least four weeks in advance. Sites like Writing.ShawGuides.com, AALBC.com, and DaytonLit.com allow authors to submit literary events.

Write a media release. If you're not proficient in creating this marketing copy, consider hiring freelance talent from Fiverr.com, TextBroker.com, or UpWork.com. You provide the theme, keywords, and desired outcome. You can submit the media releases to paid and free eblast services. Email me at info@penofthewriter.com with Do It Right Media Release Help in the subject line. I'll send you examples of media releases I wrote that landed front-page, above-the-crease, full-color articles…FREE!

News outlets want content that spotlights positivity in their community. Contacting local media for interviews or articles can attract new fans. Consider radio, TV, newspaper, and magazines. When I hosted a book signing for my granddaughter, I researched Atlanta's major news outlets, found emails of producers, and sent an email notifying them of a four-year-old local author. She was featured on 11 Alive News. They posted the segment on YouTube https://youtu.be/tijbGvh2_qE. Sites like RadioGuestList.com and HelpAReporter.com connect experts like you with journalists and show hosts.

Event

Table presentation. If your display appeals to the eyes, readers will be more inclined to stop for a chat. Consider bright colors, staging in tiers, and candy. Offering a freebie (book, promotional item, etc.) is a great way to attract visitors and collect emails. Display signage with prices, show specials, and QR codes for touchless payments.

Have ample change. I cannot tell you the number of times neighboring authors have asked me for change because they weren't prepared to transact business. I round my prices to multiples of five-dollar denominations, so I don't need coins or one-dollar bills.

Accept credit cards. Many eCommerce options are available. I use Paypal.com's mobile card reader which works with my smartphone to accept credit cards. The program features are simple: the device, no contract, and a nominal transaction fee.

Engage book lovers. The table can be a place of comfort for the shy author and it can also be a barrier to connecting with your readers. Consider vendor carts at malls. Are you more likely to peruse the product of the salesperson who stands, greets you, and invites you to "check out the merchandise" or the one who sits on the stool with his back to you? Take on the persona of the salesperson who works on commission: energetic, friendly, and attentive! If they like you, they are more likely to buy from you.

Most authors don't want to feel like a pushy salesperson. Instead of selling, think of your book as providing a service. It's easier to pitch your message when your perspective is helping the reader experience transformation.

WIIFM. What's in it for me? The reader has to see value in your book. Ask a couple of open-ended questions to find out what's important to them and then align your pitch to meet that need. Keep it short and sweet. For example, I pitch my bestselling novel, *The Forbidden Secrets of the Goody Box* (TheGoodyBoxBook.com), several ways:

- For women, my spiel includes that I surveyed men and listened while they had that barbershop, locker-room, man-cave conversation, to which women aren't normally privy, to divulge relationship secrets that help women better understand men.
- For fathers of daughters, I explain that a father is the first protector of the goody box and if he wants his daughter(s) to avoid the heartache and pitfalls of bad relationship decisions, this book helps start that sometimes difficult conversation about dating and sex.
- For pastors and youth leaders, I focus on the fact that the book is a call to abstinence that complements the teachings of the Bible.

Host a contest. With every purchase, customers earn an entry for a gift card, free book, or one-on-one mentoring with you. Encourage customers to return to your table at a specific time to find out who won. You can purchase tickets or create business-card sized forms to capture name, email, and phone. You can draw a winner or use WheelOfNames.com.

Work your author celebrity. Take pictures with customers holding your book. Tip the top of it forward slightly to minimize glare. If you have a retractable banner, stand near it for added branding. Throughout the day, post those pictures to social media, tagging the event and host. Include your branded hashtags and generic ones to create a virtual thread. For example, #PenOfTheWriter #TheGoodyBoxBook #FreeYourMindWritersRetreat #PowerBookFest #DoItRightTheFirstTime #Bestseller #Author #Write #Publishing #Fiction #Nonfiction #RelationshipAdvice #Dating #EventName #CityOfEvent

At the start of the event, and throughout as time permits, I conduct Facebook Lives inviting people to the event. I put on my roving-reporter hat to interview other vendors, attendees, and the event host.

Speak. If the opportunity is available, speak at the event. Whether a panelist, presenter, or keynote, you position yourself as an expert, connect with a wider audience, and share an event-only offer to get readers to your product table. I sell more books when I deliver an informative, entertaining, and engaging presentation. The technique has landed subsequent speaking engagements and thousands of dollars in back-of-the-room sales. I encourage attendees to take pictures and share on social media with specific hashtags. This strategy gets attendees involved in magnifying and monetizing my message. The person with the most shares and/or comments wins a gift, while I win new fans, friends, and followers. I take a selfie with the audience behind me and ask them to hold up the books they purchased from me. Consider asking someone to record two-minute videos and take pictures of you standing in front of the room. These "receipts" showcase your style and confirm your expert status. Solicit video testimonials following your presentation.

Note: If you are confirmed to speak, consider having an assistant manage your product table in your absence. When I travel alone, I place an organza drape over my product so it's visible to passersby, but not as accessible. I place promotional material on top of the covering and a tent card that indicates my expected return time.

I created eight-page booklets using Publisher (two 8.5" x 11" sheets printed double-sided). The booklets include the book cover, synopsis, copyright page, reviews, first chapter, bio, and order form with contact info. I give them away at trade shows, drive-through windows, and anywhere I meet potential customers. For multi-day events, I write my booth number on the front so readers can find me later. I pique their interest with page-turning finesse, and they often come back to purchase the book. The booklets prove to be quite effective when I conduct workshops.

When I vend in expo centers, trade shows, or large open spaces, I push my product table toward the middle of the booth and put my eight-foot retractable banner on it to increase visibility. I stand at the front of my booth, on a rubber mat, and greet passersby. I invite them into "my space" and offer a seat. While they're resting, I share my books.

<u>Post-event</u>

Follow up is important. Send a thank-you email to the organizer and your new fans within forty-eight hours of the event. You can write the email in advance and save it as a draft. Once you customize the message with names of winners, team members, etc., drop in the emails (blind copy only) and send it. Sometimes, I mail a thank-you card to the host. The added touch is appreciated and memorable.

To further boost your brand and elevate your success, share the experience with your fans, friends, and followers with an eblast highlighting video testimonials, endorsements, and pictures. I use <u>ConstantContact.com</u> for communication and customer retention. Visit <u>PenOfTheWriter.com/Powerful-Affiliates</u> for savings on ConstantContact, Fiverr, QuickBooks, and more.

To be effective at book events, plan, promote, and profit. This business is not easy, but the rewards — tangible and intangible — are worth it when you do it right the first time.

Best-selling author and award-winning publisher, Valerie J. Lewis Coleman serves professional speakers and experts to magnify and monetize their message by publishing quality books. With over fifteen years of experience in the book business, she has published over 170 authors and helped thousands of writers navigate the challenges of self-publishing. This expert divulges industry secrets on avoiding the top five mistakes made by 95% of new authors, pricing your book to sell, and identifying shady publishers. Valerie hosts citywide book events, which have connected over 700 authors to avid readers. Her dynamic presentation and knowledge of the business take writers from pen to paper to published as they master self-publishing to make money! Schedule a complimentary discovery session with Valerie at https://penofthewriter.as.me.

Connect with Valerie
PenOfTheWriter.com
Amazon.com/author/valeriejlewiscoleman
Facebook.com/PenOfTheWriter
LinkedIn.com/in/PenOfTheWriter
Instagram.com/PenOfTheWriter
Twitter.com/PenOfTheWriter

Valerie's Favorite Resource
I use POWERful affiliates to simplify bookkeeping, client scheduling, and project management. Visit PenOfTheWriter.com/Powerful-Affiliates for savings that will help your business run smoother.

Valerie J. Lewis Coleman

Do It Right the First Time

Six Sensible Strategies for Selling Success

Garrett M. Carter, Ph.D.

Upon releasing my first book in 2011, I felt an incredible sense of accomplishment. My dream-turned-project of over a year had finally come to fruition. In my hand, I held a published book that started as ideas in my head. I thought I was finished; however, I soon realized that my journey as an author was far from over. I was tasked with transferring my excitement into finding ways to get family, friends, and strangers to part with their hard-earned money to invest in me and my work. I needed to get others excited, too. I am fortunate to have the support of my family, friends, and their respective networks. However, the bulk of my readers are individuals I will never meet because effective marketing requires reaching beyond your circle and extended circle.

Getting your books into the hands of strangers requires a recipe comprised of passion, hard work, dedication, creativity, networking, research, and trial and error. To celebrate my tenth anniversary as a best-selling, award-winning author, I am delighted to share six sensible strategies for selling success that I utilized in hopes of helping you achieve your goals.

Invest Your Time

When you become an author, you not only add publishing credit to your name, you create a new lane in your career path. As with any successful career, advancement requires work. Your book will not magically sell on its own. You must invest countless hours identifying your target audience, and the marketing strategies required to engage them. At a minimum, plan on devoting three or four hours each week to learn how to market and sell books within your genre. I schedule Saturday mornings as my "author work time." I have found it helpful to build this activity into my weekly routine.

A plethora of free online resources are available, but not all of them are created equal. Two websites that greatly contributed to my knowledge in book marketing are KDP.Amazon.com and Kindlepreneur.com. Fantastic books (such as this one!) are also worth the investment. I found Rob Eagar's *Sell Your Book Like Wildfire: The Writer's Guide to Marketing and Publicity* particularly useful. Continually investing time in your new role pays off by allowing you to better understand how to connect with your audience to sell books.

Network and Innovate

Think outside of the box when it comes to promoting your book and be open to routes that may increase exposure to your target audience. While most authors would love to be featured in a national newspaper or be the guest expert on a talk show, the likelihood of this happening right out of the gate is rare...if ever.

As such, it is important to network and connect with other writers and influencers. Join local, regional, and national social media groups that cater to authors. I have been featured in numerous newspapers, podcasts, and publications like *HuffPost* because I networked with those interested in my subject matter. I also participated in book expos and created opportunities to sell books.

Be innovative. Look for win-win opportunities where you and another party benefit equally. For example, I received permission to sell books at the church I attend. In turn, I donated a portion of my proceeds to our scholarship committee (a win-win). In another example, I called a manager of a retail store to see if I and two other authors could host a back-to-school book selling event. Bookstores are overwhelmed with these requests and often decline, but the manager at this office supply store happily agreed. This event provided us with an opportunity to sell books to the store's customers and the store had an opportunity to sell products to our network of supporters (a win-win). Networking and innovation will position you to take advantage of existing opportunities and enable you to create your own.

Budget for the Essentials

Since books will not magically sell themselves, a successful marketing plan requires funds. Fortunately, a little can go a long way. If you do not have money saved for marketing expenses, find ways to reduce your nonessential spending for the next few months to save several hundred dollars. In addition to having your own inventory of books, I recommend investing in business cards, postcards, and bookmarks to promote your new release. I use <u>VistaPrint.com</u>. Simplify the purchasing process for consumers by designing your marketing paraphernalia for convenience. Be sure to include websites and QR codes so potential readers can access and purchase your book quickly.

Be prepared to mail copies of your book to obtain reviews and enter contests. Some book reviews are free, while others require a fee. I utilize <u>ReadersFavorite.com</u> for free book reviews. I entered one of my nonfiction titles in their international contest and it won an award! Most book contests require an entry fee, but it is worth the chance to become an award-winning author and add an award seal to your cover.

Increasingly, authors run digital ads with Amazon, Google, and Facebook to reach potential readers. This strategy can be costly, so maximize your efficiency by doing your homework to avoid mistakes. Kindlepreneur was essential to me learning the ad game. I created ad campaigns with Amazon and Google and achieved profitability on both platforms. Digital ads are requiring greater investment, so it is important to diversify your marketing efforts. Whenever you release a title, budget for the essentials to take advantage of your new-release window and maintain your momentum.

Distribute Free Copies…Strategically

If you became an author with the goal of increasing your income, you may be questioning this strategy. However, when done strategically, distributing free copies of your book can boost sales. My nonfiction books are for educators. I sent complimentary copies to superintendents of large school districts around the country. My rationale was that at least a few superintendents would value my work, see how it benefits their teachers, and purchase copies for their districts. I was right. This move paid off.

I also provided free copies of my books to program directors and coordinators in positions to purchase in bulk. While some may advise to never give away your work, I view it as an investment. If I give away one book that I purchased at a wholesale rate of three or four dollars to an individual who purchases twenty copies at full retail price, that investment is well worth it. This win will not happen every time, which highlights the importance of identifying your audience and knowing how to reach them so your efforts are not in vain. As you prepare to release your title, understand that selling involves strategic giving.

Begin Your Next Book

After releasing my first book, a mentor and fellow author asked, "When is your next book coming out?" She was 100% serious, but that was the absolute last thing I wanted to hear after all of the time, energy, and effort I had put into my debut title. I did not know if I had it in me to go through the process again. Yet, ten years later, I have authored four fiction and four nonfiction books! You receive more bang for the buck with your marketing efforts when you have multiple books because your universe of titles supports each other. If readers purchase and enjoy one of your books, they may want more. So, it is important for you to capitalize on this opportunity. Inside my books, I include an "Also by this author" section to inform readers about my other titles. In my nonfiction texts, I include sample pages from my other books as a promotional tool. Note that having multiple books only helps when you ensure that all of your works are high quality. Do not cut corners with editing, formatting, design, and publishing because if readers are not pleased with your first book, they will not bother with the others. That said, begin writing your next masterpiece today!

Own Your Role

When I first became an author, I had to push myself to embrace my new identity. Even now, some of my acquaintances and colleagues do not know that I am an author, especially those not on social media. It is not something that I shout from the rooftops. I am cautious, perhaps overly so, about not coming off as boastful or sounding like a desperate salesman. However, there have been occasions in which being humble or not making a sales pitch resulted in missed opportunities. Owning my role as an author is about fully acknowledging that being a writer, publisher, and marketer is part of who I am. It is important that I recognize, embrace, and speak to this identity, when necessary — even if it pushes me beyond my comfort zone.

This journey has been a blessing as my books have appeared on Amazon's bestseller list in multiple categories, and I have also received multiple awards. I am not always quick to share this information, but I remind myself that owning my role as an author, including the accolades and expertise that I have gained, solidifies my position and credibility in this space and helps sell books. Remain humble but be proud of your work. Own your role as an author and celebrate your success.

Garrett M. Carter, Ph.D. is a best-selling author and award-winning educator with a passion for developing tomorrow's leaders. With over a decade of experience in education, Dr. Carter has served as a teacher and administrator in K-12 and higher education. He believes that children should not limit themselves to only one dream; instead, they should have many. He advocates to increase the diversity of main characters in children's books while enhancing the character of students in real life.

Connect with Dr. Garrett
Amazon.com/author/garrettcarterbooks
Linkedin.com/in/garrett-m-carter-ph-d-572772192

Dr. Garrett's Favorite Resource
Sell Your Book Like Wildfire: The Writer's Guide to Marketing and Publicity because it is filled with great advice and practical tips for book marketing.

Do It Right the First Time

Skyrocket Your Social Media Engagement with Nine Simple Strategies!

Queashar L. Halliburton

Congratulations! You wrote and self-published a book! You are officially an author. You are to be commended for accomplishing a significant task that many aspiring authors never achieve. Not to discourage you; however, most authors don't sell 250 copies of their book. Why? Because some authors embrace the false belief that readers will organically show up. Your ideal readers only show up when you intentionally work to market and cater to their needs. The easiest way to make that happen is with an established author platform, which many first-time authors haven't built.

An effective author platform creates a buzz for your content. It consists of all the things you do to attract your audience to your brand. It's how you implement and engage the know-like-and-trust factor. You must develop relationships with other experts in the industry and collaborate with them to bring awareness to your books' topics. Networking and collaboration help increase your visibility exponentially.

After initial book sales to family, friends, and close associates, you may be all tapped out. Now, you must get creative to develop ways to sell and market your book. First, stop hiding in shame, embarrassment, or fear! Believe me, it's okay. Come from behind your book and introduce yourself to potential readers. Know your target audience. If your book is nonfiction, think of their pain points. What things keep them up late at night? Think about their wants, needs, and aspirations, then create content to solve the problem for them. You will inspire them to connect with you emotionally and they'll come back for more!

One way to spring new life into your book marketing plan is to utilize the power of social media! When your friends share their experience with you to their friends, your audience expands. However, I don't recommend that you leave this marketing strategy to chance. It is best to develop a strategic plan of action to attract your ideal readers. To get the most attraction traction, choose the social media platforms that best reflect you, your book, and your brand.

This summary will help choose the platform that most resonates with your ideal readers:
- Facebook is one of the largest social media platforms. Users create free profiles to connect with family, friends, colleagues, and new people. You can share long-form content, photos, music, videos, and more to engage with your network.

- LinkedIn is the platform for professionals. If you want to connect with business owners, influencers, or organizers, start here.
- Twitter is a social networking site where posts—referred to as tweets—are limited to 280 characters. You friend someone by "following them." If you like someone's post, you can share or "retweet" it.
- Instagram is a fun image-driven network. You connect with family, friends, and business owners by posting photos, videos, memes, and colorful audio messages.
- Pinterest is an eye-catching exploratory app especially helpful when you need ideas to jolt your inspiration. Users attach pins to boards to keep their ideas organized and handy.
- Clubhouse is a new social audio app. Guests can network, join the stage, and collaborate on this group-style podcast. Professionals meet new clients by engaging in real-time. You can enter rooms with your favorite speakers, authors, and social media influencers to listen, learn, and discuss topics.

You can use social media sites to help build your brand, connect to your ideal reader, and drive traffic to your website. Once you know where you want to start, use these top social media strategies to grow your audience and skyrocket your engagement!

Tip #1: If you are new to social media, build one social media platform other than your website to start attracting readers. Because so many platforms are available, you can become overwhelmed trying to learn, create, and post content. Master one and then move on to the next one. Let's start with my favorite social media app, Instagram. I love Instagram because it's lively and colorful. It's like a personal internet kiosk where you express yourself and show the world your superpowers! Before you create your content, establish a business or creator profile so you can study your analytics and measure the growth of your brand. These insights summarize your account including audience reach, audience growth, content shared, and content interactions. Check it weekly to evaluate what is working, what needs to be tweaked, and what needs to be trashed.

Tip #2: Design shareable content that speaks to the needs of your tribe. Build a genuine relationship by inviting them into your world. How? By providing valuable information to help them get from point A to B. Create subject matter to educate, entertain, and skyrocket your audience's engagement.

One tool that will help establish your social media collateral is Canva.com. Canva allows you to create graphics to complement your author brand. This tool is free with an option for a paid upgrade. Even if you aren't a graphic artist, you can easily create interactive templates, images, and pictures for your social media pages. Be sure to embed your name, website (without the www. prefix), hashtags, and logo in the image to solidify your brand.

Do It Right the First Time

Use your social media content to build anticipation by dropping breadcrumbs, uncovering your journey to author. A major key to social media success is consistently posting content that speaks to the needs of your audience and sparks immediate engagement. Your goal is to convert viewers to clients. Get your audience involved by asking questions including what they want to learn about your topic. Survey your target readers and use your research to create programs that serve your tribe on a deeper level.

Tip #3: Develop a social media plan that gives directives to your audience. Be strategic with every post. One of the biggest mistakes that I made when I first started my business page on Instagram was creating content without a call-to-action. Followers liked my posts and commented that my tips were great. However, unbeknownst to me, I sabotaged my engagement because I did not guide my audience to the next step. Each post should prompt your audience to do something. The more followers like, comment, or share your post, the more likely Instagram will push out your content to other viewers. Increased engagement leads to increased visibility. An algorithm is a set of rules that defines a set of actions. Define what you want your audience to do with every post.

Increase engagement with your followers using these suggestions to make the ask:
1. Like, comment, share, or drop an emoji expressing how they feel about a post.
2. Download a value-added tip sheet or checklist.
3. Book a discovery call or strategy session with you.
4. Review your signature book and tell you how it helped them.
5. Listen to your podcast or subscribe to your YouTube channel.

If you engage with your followers and provide needed value, they will ask for the next-level transformation you provide. Guide your audience to take the next step of action by telling them what you want them to do.

An engaged audience grows your brand by converting from follower to customer to client. Train your audience to understand the value gained by investing with you; another early mistake I made. As a result, people sent direct messages for the next step without investing in my expertise; the pick-your-brain syndrome. Advise your followers to book a call to invest in the next-level transformation you offer your clients. I want you to #DoItRightTheFirstTime and avoid the headache of people taking advantage of you.

Tip #4: Establish a weekly schedule for your brand so your audience knows what to expect from you. This strategy is intuitive relationship building. For example,

- Monday Motivation: Share original or borrowed inspirational quotes or affirmations.
- Tuesday Tips: Share valuable tips that help your followers.
- Wednesday Wisdom: Provide lessons that you learned on your journey as an author or subject matter expert.
- Teaching Thursday:
    1. Show up with your book to identify essential chapter takeaways.
    2. Create a fun graphic to promote the broadcast.
    3. Create a downloadable worksheet to complement the lesson.
    4. Invite potential readers to download your worksheet.
    5. Make sure the download prompts them to subscribe to your email list and share the lesson with others.
- Fun Friday: Reveal a photo highlighting your workspace or an event that you attended. You can share photos of you enjoying life and showing a healthy balance of work and play. You can share fun facts about your life, family, or dreams.

Provide daily content that brings a wealth of knowledge to your audience. Remember to include branded graphics using your signature colors and/or theme.

Tip #5: Use Instagram Stories to build the know-like-trust-factor with your ideal readers. If you aren't a well-known influencer with thousands of fans, introduce yourself to the online community by telling your brand story. Chronicling your brand story unveils layers of your backstory and explains why your brand exists. Being vulnerable and transparent while sharing makes you relatable, therefore creating an emotional bond. This relationship-building approach reveals similarities, which influence them to join your tribe.

Try these techniques to share your brand story on Instagram:
- Share your author journey in your Instagram Stories using a comparison photo: you when you started years ago and you today.
- Create an introduction video series. Using critical aspects from your book, create five short-and-sweet videos. Short clips, one to two minutes, keep your audience attentive and intrigued to want more of your content. Use chapter titles to highlight nuggets that speak to your target audience. Post them on your main feed welcoming readers to your tribe.
- Offer helpful tips or a checklist to followers who join your email list.

Do It Right the First Time

Tip #6: Use hashtags to become discoverable by your target audience. Establishing the right hashtags categorizes your content and connects it to threads of similar content. Think of using hashtags like a keyword search. When people search for a specific hashtag, they find content that resonates with them.

Choose hashtags that represent who you are as a business owner. Choose hashtags that align with your brand and purpose. Add hashtags that deal with the transformation that your readers seek. For instance, if you are an aspiring author, then use #AspiringAuthor as a hashtag. If you want to learn how to write a book or position yourself as a book-writing expert, use #HowToWriteABook. If you're hosting an event, include hashtags for the venue, city, and state. Instagram allows up to thirty hashtags to display under your graphics or in the first comment of your post. I recommend vetting your hashtags to make sure they are not banned; otherwise, your post may be hidden from viewers. Test your hashtags regularly and change them from time-to-time. It may take time to find the best hashtags, but it's worth the investment.

I helped Valerie promote the call-for-submissions and launch of this anthology using the following hashtags: #DoItRightTheFirstTime #PenOfTheWriter #write #publish #market #books #author #anthology #bestseller #AuthorResource #AuthorAdvice. Note that spaces and special characters are not allowed. Capitalizing the first letter in each word makes the hashtag easier to read.

Tip #7: Go live on IGTV, an Instagram TV channel that is highlighted on your feed, and save your broadcast. It's like YouTube on Instagram. Create a weekly broadcast to educate, enlighten, and encourage your audience. For consistency, choose the same day and time. Give your broadcast a cool name and make branded templates on Canva to promote it.

Use your expertise and critical tips from your book to help your target audience overcome challenges. Five-to-ten-minute videos are sufficient. Keep it short and sweet because people have many distractions and short attention spans. After the end of each video, invite viewers to book a one-on-one discovery call or enroll in your webinar, which will introduce them to your next product offering.

Tip #8: Create a podcast using the ideas and content from your book.
1. Design branded graphics to promote the podcast.
2. Talk about the themes mentioned in your book and the results you get for readers.
3. Use your book's core message along with current events to interview and highlight major players who resonate with your message.
4. Use Headliner.app to share audiograms and automate posts on your feed to give viewers a sneak peek of your podcast.

5. An easy platform to create your podcast is Anchor.fm. Getting started is simple and your podcasts will be distributed on multiple platforms including Apple, Spotify, Google, and Overcast.

Tip #9: Use Instagram Reels to answer frequently asked questions about your expertise. These short, interactive clips can help grow your following and increase your visibility. Utilize trending music and popular audio clips to boost your engagement while adding a fun element to your educational videos. To avoid copyright infringement, use Instagram's built-in music library that aligns with licensing agreements associated with the network. If your post violates copyright laws, Instagram may remove it and send you a notice explaining what happened.

Want more amazing social media tips? Receive hot social media tips and publishing advice in your email weekly by going to bit.ly/ConnectWithShar. I'm happy to provide education, tools, and resources for self-published authors looking to skyrocket their literary success. Cheers to your success!

Although many abandon their goals and dreams because of fear, procrastination, and insufficient resources, Queashar L. Halliburton turns those potential setbacks into stepping stones. As CEO and founder of Queashar Detroit Publishing, LLC, her greatest success resulted from operating in her God-given gifts and purpose. Shar is a graduate of Les Brown's Power Voice System for speakers and coaches. As a certified life and professional coach, she empowers professionals to push past self-sabotaging, limiting behaviors to excel in life and business. Along with serving as a member of Black Speakers Network and the Nonfiction Authors Association, Shar is a contributing writer of *Advance Magazine*, *Publish Magazine*, and the author of *Skyrocket Your Success! 10 Keys to Refocus, Reposition & Reclaim Your Purpose*!

Connect with Shar
SharHalliburton.com
amazon.com/author/queasharhalliburton
Facebook.com/qdpublishing
Linkedin.com/in/queasharhalliburton
Instagram.com/qdpublishing
Twitter.com/qdpublishing

Shar's Favorite Resource
Entrepreneur Secrets: The New Rules of Wealth Creation by Charlotte Howard. This book breaks down writing, publishing, and how to scale your book business beyond six figures.

Do It Right the First Time

Don't Reinvent the Wheel, Repurpose Your Content

Monique A. Chandler

Throughout my childhood, journaling was my outlet. Scribbling my emotions across the page allowed me the freedom to express my feelings and not break down when life spiraled out of control. Every night before bed, I wrote about my day—in all transparency—unaware that I was preparing myself to become an author.

As an adult, I had the opportunity to be the publicist for Author Nikki Rashan. My initial focus was marketing; however, that changed when Nikki read a few of my journals between book signings at an event in Dallas, Texas. Impressed with my powerful prose, she suggested that I repurpose my candid journal entries into material for a book and teach others to discover a happy place to embrace joyful memories. After receiving her sound advice, I jumped into action. I sorted through 1,400 journals I amassed over the years. Stressing the importance of having my work professionally edited to make the conversion from journals to books seamless, on January 1, 2015, Nikki advised me to connect with Joylynn M. Ross, CEO of Path to Publishing, for editing and self-publishing guidance. I was fortunate to have someone in my corner who graciously let me know that it's best — and less costly — to invest in your intellectual property on the front end than on the back end.

I promised Nikki I wouldn't haphazardly throw my intellectual property out there on my own, so I emailed Joylynn days after we spoke. Although I didn't know Joylynn personally, I trusted Nikki. And guess what. Nikki's recommendation was on the money! Joylynn patiently worked with me through my literary needs, and I signed a contract. The next day, my heart was shattered to receive the call that at forty-two, Nikki Rashan Jenkins died of complications from breast cancer. May 4, 2015 will forever be engraved in my heart. Though the void remains, I take solace in knowing I fulfilled my last promise to Nikki. For that, I am grateful.

I quickly learned that hiring a professional editor can be one of the most expensive price tags of the writing and publishing journey; however, it's also one of the most rewarding. Had I known how powerful my stories would be to others, I wouldn't have allowed my journals to sit idle for so many years. Think about what you've done. Your experiences, accomplishments, and failures. What problem would your story solve for others? Tell your story, change the world. Don't make excuses. Whatever it takes, make it happen as quickly as you can.

The costliest mistake I made was giving away my hard-earned money listening to the wrong people. I wasted over $20,000 in a single year breaking my neck attending conferences that ultimately didn't bring me any value. There was absolutely no return on the mega investment because I followed the wrong people. As a result, I regretfully made one grave mistake after another. It's okay to be a follower, but you have to make sure you're following the right people! After beating myself up for entertaining voices who were more about increasing their bottom line than helping me reach my dreams and goals, I went back to the basics of what I knew: marketing, networking, and net-weaving. My best interest may not have ever hit their radar, but I knew no one could bless my business the way I could.

Time to regroup. I paused everything for a few months to get it done. During my sabbatical, I immersed myself in research, which led to creating a marketing plan to push me closer to my professional goals. I discovered that I needed to add more "p's" to my strategies. I created a pie chart, implementing the below categories to help propel me to my next:

- Passion
- Product
- Promotion
- Packaging
- Positioning
- Pricing
- People
- Permission
- Publicity
- Pass-along

Be sure to maximize your "p's" and minimize your time. This strategy allows you to make money while you sleep. Passive income is some of the best income.

Once my marketing pie chart was completed, doors for *Reconnecting with Your Happy* opened! I had my own blend of ginger peachy black tea, coffee mugs, t-shirts, and bookmarks. I took one book and turned it into a thriving business. From penning a chapter about grief and purpose titled *The Game Changer*, to repurposing that chapter for an anthology submission with eighty-nine co-authors, to becoming an international, Amazon best-selling author for *Finding Joy in the Journey*, Volume 1, I was proof that no matter the size of the entry, publishing works wonders. I submitted that same chapter to the *Confinement Chronicles Audiobook Collection* with Angie Bee Productions. Most recently, using the same chapter, I created an eBook that sold over 500 copies to funeral homes.

Implementing the pie chart in my professional plan helped me see the endless marketing possibilities at my disposal. There's enough pie for all of us to have our own. Why settle for a slice?

Another option would be to repurpose your published works to add to your bottom line. Start with what you already know. Following this method, I devised a list of over 200 people I knew who lost a sibling. I texted them a link, including pertinent information on why my book was necessary, and how they could access it. From there, I created a workshop centered on the repurposed chapter, *The Game Changer,* and presented it to groups of individuals who had experienced sibling loss.

Look around. What resources are readily available to you? Expand your reach. Take advantage of free resources such as your local library and social media to build your audience.

Consider participating in two complimentary events each year. Be strategic to ensure you are positioned in front of your ideal audience who wants and needs what you offer. On these occasions, you are not paid a speaking fee; however, a product table is provided to you at no cost. When executed properly, you can build your following while generating significant back-of-the-room sales.

Create fundraisers and a pre-order campaign six months prior to your book launch to jumpstart your book business. Instead of getting in debt or asking close family and friends to drain their bank accounts, create a contribution campaign requesting 1000 people to make a $10 contribution.

You've got this, and the world needs what you've got!

Distinguished Toastmaster Monique A. Chandler possesses a unique blend of contagious, high volume, motivational energy, and a sincere heart for helping others reach their pinnacle. As an international best-selling author, consultant, and educator, she influences others to reconnect with their happy. Chandler is an experienced professional consultant with an emphasis in social media management and sales and marketing. She is a bridge for teenagers transitioning to college and helps their parents secure education funding. She serves homeless female veterans to transition back into society by preparing for interviews, developing organizational and communication skills, and improving esteem.

Connect with Monique
ReconnectingWithYourHappy.com
Facebook.com/ReconnectingWithYourHappy
Instagram.com/ReconnectingWithYourHappy
Twitter.com/MotivatingMo

Monique's Favorite Resource
Path to Publishing Literary Blueprint is my absolute favorite author resource because it teaches you step-by-step how to navigate publishing without a presenter in front of you. This resource taught me how to create multiple streams of income. I have also been able to maximize my time and minimize my efforts by applying for grants and all-expenses-paid fellowship opportunities. PathToPublishing.com

Do It Right the First Time
Seven Tips to Speak to Sell!

Andrea Foy

I wrote my first book, *Hire Power: How to Find, Get, and Keep a Job*, published by QueenVPublishing.com, in 2010. I never considered speaking to promote my book because I am an introvert. I was terrified of speaking in front of people, but I managed to survive a few book signings. Authors read from their books, talked about the publishing process, answered questions. I did not.

Social media marketing was still a new concept for me. I set up profiles for the sole purpose of promoting *Hire Power*. I made Animoto.com videos and shared them on LinkedIn, Facebook, Twitter, Pinterest, and Instagram with excerpts and the front cover. People contacted me to buy my book. Then, the unexpected happened. I received an email, asking if I could speak to a local youth group about job hunting. I deleted it without even reading it all. I was not about to stand in front of a room of people to do a speech about my book.

A few weeks later, I received another email that changed my life. The organizer wrote, "How much do you charge to do a presentation, and can we buy copies of your book?" I could not delete that email. I was scared, not crazy! I needed to do something fast because I had left more than enough money on the table.

I was familiar with Toastmasters International, the largest global speaking organization. I knew that people participated to learn how to speak better. I found a club close to where I worked. My plan was to attend the meeting and buy a tape or book about speaking. I had no plans to speak, mind you, but to *learn* how to speak. Imagine my horror when I realized that I had to learn to speak…by doing it live in front of people!

My first speech was a disaster. I stood in a small room, half full of people, staring at the ceiling. As I gripped the podium, I prayed that God would rip open the roof and kill me, right then and there! One club member recorded my speech and emailed it to me. I tried to watch, but I couldn't. I could not hear myself talking because I mumbled, babbled, and trembled. No more public speaking for me. If I could not sell my book, which I had spent so much time and effort on, through social media and a few book signings, so be it! I was ready to give up my dream of being an author when I realized it involved talking.

Instead of quitting, I chose to redeem myself. I wrote a speech, "Personal Safety for Women," where I reflected on my career as a flight attendant and how I overcame my fear of traveling alone. The club members commented on how they had never thought of the tips I mentioned. Some of the men said that they would tell women in their lives about the recommendations. The women took notes. I was onto something.

Do It Right the First Time

The following week, I gave the speech, "Personal Safety, Part Deux." My club members were complimentary, suggesting that I write a book on travel safety. I did not think that I had enough material to write a book, but I gave more information every time I spoke. I finished the first ten speeches needed to earn the designation of competent communicator. The recognition boosted my confidence. I did a few presentations to small groups in my church and around town.

A few months later, I received an email from the CEO of the Professional Woman Network (PWN). She saw my posts on LinkedIn about *Hire Power*. She was compiling an anthology, *Single and Loving It: An African American Woman's Guide to Life* and wanted me to contribute a chapter. I mentioned the tips that were so popular with my Toastmasters club. She loved the idea and requested a ten-page chapter. I wrote and submitted *Personal Safety for the Single Woman*. A few months after the anthology released, the compiler recommended expanding the chapter into a book. The result was *In the Still of the Night: Personal Safety for Women.*

A few months after my third book released (two books and one anthology), she asked me to present at the PWN International Women's Conference. Although I was reasonably comfortable speaking in public, an international conference was entirely different. I started to turn down the invitation, but my publisher said, "Stick with Toastmasters, and you'll be ready." I went back to my club ignited by the goal to present to an international audience. The summer of 2013, I gave a thirty-minute presentation on safety tips to more than a hundred women.

Toastmasters was one of the best things I ever did for my writing career. I created a keynote, "Personal Safety for Women," and conducted seminars and presentations. I practiced to be comfortable and natural when I spoke. I submitted a story to a Toastmasters' anthology and was selected to present at their international conference. I could not feel my legs while I was on stage, but I spoke to an audience of 1,200 people! And to think, it all started with a speech.

To date, my favorite speaking experience was in 2017 when I spoke at *Purple Reign: An Interdisciplinary Conference on the Life and Legacy of Prince Rogers Nelson* in Manchester, United Kingdom. My speech was based on my memoir, *Prince and Me: His #1 Fan, My Minneapolis Memories.* Imagine. In seven years, I went from praying to die at the podium to presenting in the United Kingdom! You can do it. I am living proof.

My experience with speaking to sell books has worked well for me. These seven tips will help you get started.

1. **Toastmasters!** I hope my story intrigued you enough to consider joining a club. Even if you are not nervous about public speaking, the organization can help you improve your speaking skills, develop and present ideas more effectively, and gain confidence. A good club can help you hone the message of your

book. I learned how to host workshops and seminars. Toastmasters meetings have a Table Topics segment where we practice answering impromptu questions like "What is your book about?" or "Why should I buy it?" I was able to practice the answers. The feedback from my club members was invaluable, shaping and sharpening my content. Type your zip code in the Find a Club box at Toastmasters.org. Visit clubs to see which ones are inviting to you. You do not have to join or speak right away. Take your time and ease into it.

2. **Practice everywhere.** One of my Toastmasters mentors spoke anywhere he could to perfect his speech and overcome his fear of public speaking. He went to senior centers, nursing homes, colleges, and churches, sharing content with a willing audience. Sometimes he donated books or offered a discount. He said that his audience gave him invaluable feedback about his topic, information, resources, and even leads! Practice to test the quality of your content and speech.

3. **Seminars and workshops**. Develop a seminar based on the content of your book. My experiences as a flight attendant qualified me as an expert on personal safety. I developed seminars inviting women to share their experiences and tips. Every session was different and unique. Women related to my

subject. They felt included and shared incredible stories and information. Women who came as strangers left as friends. Write about what you know. It makes speaking more enjoyable, which helps you authentically connect with your audience. Seminars are an excellent way to share your book with your niche market and make money.

4. **Book signings.** You don't have to rely on a bookstore for a signing event. Book your event and take it to the next level. Try libraries, meeting centers, and schools. Develop a short speech to discuss your book and entertain your audience. Make it interactive. Ask questions, tie in current events, if applicable. Give away books based on participation. This strategy will make your event more exciting and fun than just signing books. I used stories I uncovered in my seminars to reinforce my tips. The new material made my events unique and special.

5. **Back-of-the-room sales.** Speaking helps market and sell books. After my PWN and Toastmasters presentations, I sold and autographed books. When you confirm a speaking engagement, ask the organizer to provide a product table for you. Bring your books, cash for change, and a credit card reader. If the organizer doesn't allow selling, make sure you are allowed to mention your

book and website. Let guests know that you will be available after the event to answer questions and be sure to get emails. For the Prince Conference, which was not a book event, I carried my books in a tote bag for people who wanted copies. Speaking engagements can also generate post-event sales with online retailers, local bookstores, and libraries when audience members request your book.

6. **Speak virtually.** As of 2020, we live in a virtual world. Although we are returning to pre-pandemic routines, many speaking events are still held online. Virtual speaking allows you to reach a global audience. Explore these ideas:
    - Social media – Conduct Facebook Lives to connect with event organizers, book clubs, and readers. Provide weekly video promotions, posts, and so much more.
    - Podcasts – Be a guest or host a podcast about your book, industry, or niche.
    - YouTube – Create videos about your book, niche, or subject. People have 24-7 access to your channel and videos can go viral if enough people view them. One good video can go a long way.
7. **Be like John.** One of my heroes and mentors, Dr. John C. Maxwell, is the world's leading expert on leadership. With over 30 million books sold, he is also a phenomenal speaker.

He taught and certified me to be a leadership speaker. He releases a book; it becomes a bestseller. His book, *Change the World*, released in 2020. During the global pandemic, John was forced to cancel his scheduled book tour. His travel itinerary included hotels, meals, and transportation for him and his staff. His team suggested that he do a Facebook Live to debut his book. Not convinced that Facebook was the way to go, he agreed to try. The event garnered over 12,000 live views (I was one of them)! He reached thousands of people worldwide, and he didn't have to leave home. His virtual tour was far more successful than his in-person tour would have ever been. To date, he still hosts a Monday Facebook Live at noon. He discovered a new way to connect with his audience.

There you have it—seven tips on speaking to sell your book. It works for me, it works for John Maxwell, and I am confident that it will work for you. Speak to sell!

Andrea Foy is an international author, speaker, and coach. She is a Distinguished Toastmaster with Toastmasters International, the leading speaking organization in the world. She was honored to speak on stage at the international convention and contributed to the organization's first anthology. Andrea is a certified women's empowerment coach with the Professional Woman Network. She conducted presentations for the organization and co-authored several projects. As a certified John C. Maxwell speaker, coach, and trainer, she trained with her mentor and an elite team of world-renowned coaches including motivational speaker, Les Brown. Andrea's favorite professional accomplishment is speaking at the first Interdisciplinary Prince Conference in Manchester, UK. She has written and published four books and coauthored fifteen anthologies.

Connect with Andrea
AndreaFoy.com
Facebook.com/afoy1
Linkedin.com/in/AndreaFoy
Instagram.com/Mkafoy
Twitter.com/andreafoy2020

Andrea's Favorite Resource
Kindle Direct Publishing (KDP.Amazon.com) because it gives the freedom to publish yourself.

Valerie J. Lewis Coleman

Do It Right the First Time

Generating Multiple Streams of Income from Your Book

Denise M. Walker

Expand beyond is how you must think when it comes to authorship. In this chapter, I provide you with ways to build upon your book and do it right the first time.

When I began writing, I had no clue as to what I was doing. I published my first book and assumed my work was done. Wrong! As an educator, I plan, research, analyze, gather resources, and execute. I must deliver lessons so my students can grasp the standards presented. Over the past five years, I learned to incorporate my teaching background in my business.

You may be asking, "What does that have to do with writing?" Lots. I learned to see each of my books as a resource to be presented in various ways. Just as students learn differently, so do your readers. Some consume the information by reading it, whereas others need to listen to the audio. Still others need it presented with a hands-on approach such as a workshop. Yes, you must see your book as multiple streams of income. Not only your books, but your gifts and talents are potential streams as well.

Educators create weekly lesson plans. You should develop a written plan on how to present your books to potential readers. If you are serious about turning your authorship into a business, you must plan how to use your skills to grow and make money.

I often hear successful entrepreneurs say, "You can be your own boss and develop your own schedule." I never understood the fullness of their words until I launched my business. Stick with me as I share tips on how to see the value in your book and yourself.

First, determine your audience. No, your audience is not everyone. That's too broad. Think about who you are trying to reach with your message by defining your purpose for writing this book.

After determining your audience, research their needs, wants, and pain points. For example, one of my target audiences is "at-promise" teen girls who need encouragement, empowerment, and mentoring. I pulled themes from my book including choosing friends wisely, loving yourself first, and your pain is not your identity, and developed mentoring workshops. Did I mention the book I'm referencing is fiction? Yes, you can pull content from fiction or nonfiction.

After developing workshop topics, I reached out to youth mentors and youth ministry leaders. I shared my proposal for the workshops, and they scheduled me to present to their teen girls. Note: This step requires flexibility. When I arrived to one session, I realized that some girls were much younger than expected. Initially, I was stumped, but I made adjustments as I presented. One of those younger babies was the highlight of my eight-week session.

She shared that she had learned so much by being with the older girls and read poems she had written.

Determine your territory. Do you want to reach schools or churches? Are you called to a local, national, or international audience? Your territory may not unfold upfront; however, think about it now. Because I also write for women who have experienced trauma, my territory is far-reaching. I have presented at virtual and in-person events. I hosted my own online events via Zoom and traveled beyond my home state. The more you break down the components of your book, the more you will see how to expand your message and income potential.

Another expansion strategy is teaching others how to use your book in their business, ministry, or mentoring group. I signed up to be a presenter at the Christian Book Lovers Retreat. I had to wait for approval and was a nervous wreck. Once accepted, I decided to present as I did in my classroom. I pulled a passage from the Bible and the group read it together. I demonstrated how to use a Bible-literacy strategy from one of my books, then allowed the ladies to explore different strategies. They had to apply the same Scripture to each strategy as they rotated around the room. The energy was high, feedback was amazing, and I sold all of my journals. Because the ladies shared what they'd learned, other individuals purchased my product. Did I happen to mention that I am an introvert? If I can do it, so can you.

Let's shift to you as an individual. Think about your success. I'm not referring to fortune or fame. What are you successful at doing that helps others? Are you good at drawing? Are you good at math? Do you create or design things? At what one thing are you gifted? What do you love so much that you will do it for free? I love teaching others and have lots of writing and reading training. I had to understand that the gift was already there. But how was it going to generate income?

I began copy editing for authors of children's books. I connected with other copyeditors and people who needed my service. I invested in more resources and training. As I coached authors of children's books and nonfiction, my teaching skills kicked in automatically. I helped authors develop their thoughts, one step at a time. I realized it is something I love, and it is the top income generator for my business.

Another means of seeing your success is by looking at ways you enjoy helping others. It doesn't always have to be about money. You can build relationships that can take you places your money can't. That relationship can grow into a great friendship, one you can call on in time of need. As a Christian book club host and podcaster, I built priceless relationships with the authors and individuals I interviewed. While assisting them to share their work, ministry, and business, I get the opportunity to grow my own. We use platforms like Clubhouse to have discussions. People listen, and we share how to connect with us. Just like that, I gained potential clients without pushing my services.

I pray these strategies and examples will assist you to stretch the content of your book. Over the years, I watched it unfold like a puzzle. When I was afraid, I did it afraid. When I didn't know, I learned. When it didn't work, I tried again. It's a trial-and-error process, but you will never make it through the process if you stop at the book. You have so much inside you and far more greatness beyond the pages of your book. Your audience is waiting for you!

I leave you with empowering words from my father, who is now deceased.

> "Never allow anyone to tell you what you can't become but know that nothing good comes easy. It takes work and perseverance."

You have it within you. Now develop tunnel vision, go forth, and expand your reach.

Denise M. Walker is busy broadcasting Christ and Christian literature. She hosts workshops, *Hope in Christ with Denise* podcast, and offers publishing services through Armor of Hope Writing & Publishing. In addition to a blog, Denise facilitates Hope-in-Christ Book Club. For over twenty years, she served as a Language Arts and reading teacher for elementary and middle school students. Denise has penned six books, three of which are bestsellers. Since 2016, she has served as a writing coach and copyeditor of children's and nonfiction books.

Connect with Denise
DeniseMWalker.com
Amazon.com/author/denisew
Facebook.com/authordenisemwalker
Linkedin.com/in/author-denise-m-walker-b8180960
Instagram.com/authordenisemwalker
Twitter.com/author_denise

Denise's Favorite Resource
I love Scrivener.com because it helps me organize my stories and import the websites I need.

Do It Right the First Time

Building Brand, Bridges, and Book Sales

Noni Banks

According to *Merriam-Webster Dictionary*, branding is "the promotion of a product or service by identifying it with a particular brand." I define branding as the story you communicate to the world. Your brand is the signature way you create an emotional connection with your readers. Branding is like a magnet that allows you to attract customers, opportunities, and income. Effective branding informs your readers that you have the solution to their problem or information to satisfy a need. Understanding who you are as a brand, also known as your brand identity, allows you to effectively reach your readers.

Defining your brand starts with your why. As a serial entrepreneur who worked a full-time job, I struggled to find a community that addressed my specific needs. The Diva Movement was created to fill the void by empowering, motivating, and inspiring women entrepreneurs to move confidently toward their dreams. My goal is to provide support, tools, and resources to help grow and market their businesses with confidence. It's been said that you should be able to communicate your brand in six words or less. "We help women entrepreneurs win!"

Your brand is not for everyone, so the next step is to know, understand, and reach your audience. If you build a brand by trying to target everyone, you will miss the opportunity to reach your ideal reader. The Diva Movement serves women who work a "9-to-5" while running a business. Having a clearly defined audience has allowed our brand to connect with this demographic.

How I built my Facebook community to 19,000+ fans, friends, and followers

I started with lofty marketing goals. I had to become an expert of the platforms that I planned to use to reach my audience. I learned everything I could about how to maximize my social media presence. I spent years listening to my ideal audience and studying post-performance, interactions, and other social media analytics.

As they say, "Content is king." Creating engaging content was critical to the growth of my social media community. Followers crave a variety of content, from informative to entertaining. Here's the thing, if you are not writing content that is purposeful and relevant to your audience, you will not convert them to customers. Creating Facebook groups helped build community for our female entrepreneurs because they were engaged in meaningful conversations and connections. What happens when you find a great place to hang out? You share it! You want your fans to recruit more fans, so engagement is key. Many theories exist about Facebook and Instagram algorithms, but it comes down to this: If people are saving, sharing, commenting, and liking your posts, the algorithms determine that more people should see them. And this, my friend, moves you higher in the algorithm ranking!

I launched my company on Facebook. Six years later, Facebook headquarters recognized my efforts and appointed me to the Small Business Council to help empower small business owners. This acknowledgment proved that I was on to something.

How I keep my tribe engaged

Relationships matter. Your network is your net worth. Building genuine relationships is a critical factor in the growth and expansion of my company. My approach has always been to add value to every relationship, which allowed me to build a vast and diverse network. As with any great relationship, you have to cultivate it and understand the other person's needs. The same applies to the customers you serve. It's essential to stay relevant and keep them engaged.

Here are my top tips to keep your audience engaged:
- Be yourself. People are looking for authenticity. Your audience wants to see the real you, so let your personality shine. Allow your audience to get to know your company and the person behind the brand.

- Tell your story. Everyone loves a great story. Learn how to tell your story in a compelling and interesting way to boost engagement.
- Have a conversation. Communication should not be one-sided. Learn how to have quality conversations with your audience. Be responsive to questions, comments, and direct messages from them.
- Be consistent. Consistency is key across every aspect of your business. Writing an occasional blog, posting once a month, or sending a random email will not keep an audience engaged. Set a goal for how often you will engage with your audience and stay consistent.

How I monetize my message on social media

I utilize Shops on Facebook and Instagram to sell digital marketing products. I promote these products and purchase ads on my top platforms. I target my message and audience based on the goals of the ad campaign. You can review high-performing posts and retarget your audience with social media ads. This tool is very powerful when used correctly.

Hosting live streams on Facebook and Instagram helps generate leads for our coaching and social media management services.

As a result of growing my audience, I receive influencer offers from various companies. I share great products with my fans, friends, and followers while generating income. The companies win, my audience wins, and I win!

Note: Directing people to your website is a fundamental business strategy that puts you one step closer to your customers. However, most new authors miss this opportunity because they use social media and Amazon as personal websites.

How my background in public relations helps me market

For much of my college and early professional career, I worked closely with the media. From writing for a newspaper, operating behind the camera, and featured in front of it, these foundational experiences demonstrated how to work with the media to achieve my marketing goals. My background helped me understand how to define, research, and reach my target market. It also helped me learn and practice the art of building brand awareness.

A significant part of public relations involves building a brand image and sharing your message to the community, stakeholders, and the public. Public relations focuses on building, cultivating, and maintaining the connection between the public and the business. I expanded my network across corporate, nonprofit, and community arenas, which proved priceless when I launched The Diva Movement. Nurturing relationships built bridges that accelerated my business growth.

Events are a big part of public relations. I coordinated and spearheaded national and statewide events. Today, my company hosts eight to ten events per year. Leveraging events as a marketing tool helped The Diva Movement expand.

Three things to optimize your social media effectiveness

Many business owners feel overwhelmed with social media. However, when used effectively, social media can be a powerful tool to grow your brand, gain new customers, and increase revenue.

Before you get started, set goals for what you want to achieve on social media. Common goals include increasing brand awareness, generating more leads, and driving traffic to your website.

Decide how you will measure your success. If it matters, it needs to be measured. Common ways to measure your social goals are conversion rates, engagement rates, and the number of visitors to your website. I encourage you to research which social media platform your target audience most uses and focus on that platform. As your confidence increases, add a platform and repeat the process.

Implement these tips to get started:
- Be Authentic. It's important to give people a taste of who you are and what your company represents. Be real. The more "unfiltered" you can be, the more likely people are to relate and engage with you and your content.

- Schedule everything. You can plan and schedule your content on many platforms. This strategy allows you to be intentional about what and when you're posting. Some platforms provide additional benefits like the best time to post and hashtag strategies. Schedule time to create content, also known as content batching, which keeps you focused and saves time.
- Repurpose content. This tip is one of my favorite social media hacks. Repurposing content helps you have consistent messaging, improves your search engine optimization (SEO), increases your reach, and boosts your credibility. As an author, you already have content. Take an excerpt from your book and repurpose it into a blog post. Take that same excerpt and make a video. The goal is to get your content in the hands of more people, not create new content every day.

Not having a solid marketing plan is the biggest challenge for authors and individuals who desire to grow their brand. Developing sound marketing and social media strategies can be a challenge, but it doesn't have to be a struggle. Start with the end in mind. Determine your ultimate goal for using social media.

The Diva Movement helps women entrepreneurs develop a plan of action to reach these goals. We help authors understand how to market and sell product by creating messages that connect with their audience.

As an author, you wear many hats, and marketing is one of the most important. Learning how to market can be a full-time job, but don't worry. Our team can assist you.

Noni Banks is a social media/marketing coach, content creator, and CEO of The Diva Movement. The Diva Movement provides business coaching, business development training, and support to female entrepreneurs. Noni is an active community member who has served on numerous boards including The African American Chamber of Commerce, The MLK Women's Service Board, and Board of Directors for Focus Learning Charter Schools. Noni is a member of The Columbus Chamber of Commerce, NAACP, and Women for Economic and Leadership Development (WELD) Ohio. Noni has a bachelor's degree in public relations from Otterbein University.

Connect with Noni
TheDivaMovement.org
Facebook.com/TheDivaMovementInc
LinkedIn.com/in/NoniBanks
Instagram.com/TheDivaMovementInc
Twitter.com/DivaMovementInc

Noni's Favorite Resource
Canva.com is a graphic design platform used to create social media graphics, presentations, posters, documents, and other visual content. This app has hundreds of templates, images, and design elements for every industry. Canva will help you create consistent, comprehensive, and on-brand marketing materials. It's like having a graphic design team at your fingertips.

Valerie J. Lewis Coleman

Do It Right the First Time

How I Sold Over 100,000 Copies of My Children's Book...and Ways You Can Do It, Too!

Joylynn M. Ross

Yes, it's true: I sold over 100,000 copies of my children's book, *The Secret Olivia Told Me* (as N. Joy).

Although this achievement is all kinds of awesome and pretty darn extraordinary by industry standards, had I been equipped with the invaluable knowledge I've amassed after spending over two decades in the literary industry, I know for sure I could have sold ten times that amount. Learning the tricks of being successful in the literary trade, along with creating and implementing techniques and tactics of my own, would've helped Olivia's story soar even higher. However, as the literary legend Maya Angelou stated, "When you know better, you do better." *Knowing better* means it's not too late for me to double or even triple those sales. And with the information, systems, and strategies I share with you below, you can *do better* and multiply your sales, too.

But before we get started...

Now that you've Googled my children's book (and you should), you're probably saying, "But Joylynn, that book is over a decade old." True, my fellow literary artist. As we know, the literary industry deems books old after only three-to-six months on the shelf. But that's what's so great about children's books—they have the shelf life of a Twinkie or longer. Besides, even an old book is new to the person who has never read it, right? So, now that I've removed that mustard-sized seed of doubt from that creative mind of yours, let's get started!

As a literary consultant, publishing coach, and one of the best literary educators in the industry (it ain't bragging when you can back it up...with results), one of the things I share with my clients who are children's, middle-grade, and young adult authors is the benefit of becoming a vendor with their local public school system. Because it can be a time-consuming process that requires several steps, start doing your due diligence now so that you won't be caught building the plane while trying to fly it. In other words, learn as much about the systems and processes before even thinking about filling out the required applications and paperwork, or connecting with the people who can help make it happen.

Learn as much as you can about your areas of interest. Maximizing your efforts to educate yourself minimizes the instruction period and, most importantly, shortens your learning curve. It also shows the individuals you may need to chauffeur you on this journey that you're willing to get out and put gas in the car.

Quick break: I don't intend for you to perform every single task I share to get closer to your goal of selling over 100,000 copies of your children's book (or whatever goals you've set for yourself); however, I encourage you to do what unequivocally lines up with your literary dreams, visions, and goals. This is why it's crucial to work with a literary consultant or publishing coach to create a solid plan and path that avoids unnecessary tasks, expenses, and pitfalls.

Regardless of what genre you write, starting out locally regarding marketing, promoting, connecting, and collaborating is key. Just as aligning with your local public school system is crucial to your literary success, connecting with local libraries can also boost your career.

Who doesn't remember sitting with legs crossed on that nice, comfy rug that proudly boasted a colorful array of ABC and 123 blocks during story time at the library? Listening intently and watching in awe as the author sat way up high in that grown-up chair, looking like a literary rock star as they read from their book. Let's be honest, that precious library time was one of the things that ignited you to write your own books, right? Even if it wasn't, imagine you could spark a child's interest in taking the book world by storm. Your books aren't regulated to only your heart; they have the potential to live in the hearts of others as well. Just imagine, what you may have thought was a simple story can entertain, inspire, and jumpstart careers for you and others. So, hop to it! Contact your local libraries (or the library where you may be vacationing, or in town for a family reunion, etc.) and request to be included on their events calendar. Once you secure a spot, be sure to share your appearance with the local schools/school system.

Speaking of schools, allow me to circle back. You aren't required to be a vendor to host classroom workshops, do a school library takeover, etc. When it comes to school visits, it's normal to only want to hit up the librarian, principal, or reading and English teachers, but don't forget about the PTA and PTO. Do you know how many candy bars and candles they have to sell to bring in a featured author? Don't let their efforts be in vain.

Regardless of their genre, hosting book readings and author visits in a bookstore is every author's dream; however, my clients know that I do not allow them to promote *book readings, book signings,* or *author visits*. Whew, I just fell asleep typing those boring words! And if you fell asleep reading them, wake up or risk missing this crucial strategy to help you sell more of your children's books.

Don't plan stuffy author events; instead, create literary experiences! I train my clients to create catchy names and bold themes for the literary experiences they host. Then, we dive into great detail, brainstorming and creating content to market and promote the experience. Our teamwork results in sold-out affairs, lots of book sales, and attendees who can't wait to share on social media the experience that was created for them, using the hashtag generated explicitly for the event. That's a whole lot cheaper than taking out social media ads!

In my book, *Act Like an Author, Think Like a Business: Ways to Achieve Financial Literary Success*, I share the following: Are you an author of children's books? If so, make sure you market to in-home childcare providers and childcare facilities. Childcare providers love hosting "book parties" in their homes for the children they care for. Whether it's in their living room or a backyard picnic, it's a wonderful opportunity for you. Typically, they not only pay an author appearance fee, but they'll also purchase a copy of the book for each child to take home. And, of course, they'll purchase one for their home. Some providers only purchase a copy for themselves but encourage parents to purchase copies for their kiddos.

Childcare facilities love doing that extra something special for the children under their care by hosting authors because it's great for marketing and promotions on their end. Parents are most attracted to childcare facilities that provide educational experiences for their children. What says "we care about your child's education" more than hosting a book party with the author in attendance? So do your research. Contact in-home childcare providers and childcare facilities and pitch your book party.

I include dozens and dozens more ways to make money with your books in *Act Like an Author, Think Like a Business: Ways to Achieve Financial Literary Success*. But what I want you to get from the above passage is to remember that children aren't the ones buying the books; the adults are. Parents, guardians, aunts, uncles, grandparents, and teachers buy children's books for their classrooms and homes. Even tutors purchase books for their students. I can go on and on, but like I tell my clients, readers aren't your only customers, and they're certainly not the only ones who buy books...book buyers buy books! It's crucial to your book sales that you understand this.

Sure, there are steps involved in implementing and executing my suggestions. For example, connecting your school appearance to a fundraiser for the school. Believe me, I have way more trade secrets I could share with you, but that wouldn't leave room for my fellow colleagues in this book to share their amazing expertise. So, don't hesitate to connect with me to help chauffeur you along your literary journey, with the final destination being writing and publishing success. Regardless of your book's genre or the path you choose to publish your book; I am confident that we can make it happen.

Earlier I mentioned that when you know better, you do better. The keyword is *do*. The information I've shared in my chapter and the information my co-authors have shared in theirs won't work unless you *do* something with it. Real talk: It ain't gon' work unless you work it. So, what are you waiting for? Get to work!

P.S. Play groups, indoor gyms, and playgrounds (trampoline parks), candy stores, children's museums, ice cream shops, and parks and recreation centers are just a few more places and organizations to consider partnering with to sell more of your children's books.

If you need help with the book writing and publishing process, regardless of where you are on your literary journey or which path to publication you choose, award-winning and national best-selling author, Joylynn M. Ross (writing as BLESSEDselling Author E. N. Joy), and her team of experts and literary industry professionals can chauffeur you along your journey. With an over two-decade career in the literary industry, Joylynn has traditionally and self-published over forty books. She's helped thousands of authors reach their measure of literary and financial literary success as a literary consultant, publishing coach, and curriculum creator for the annual Act Like an Author, Think Like a Business conference. As a literary agent, Joylynn landed clients book deals with major and independent publishing houses. Joylynn is CEO of Path to Publishing, an author assistance company and literary service provider.

Connect with Joylynn
PathToPublishing.com
Amazon.com/author/blessedsellingauthorenjoy
Facebook.com/JoylynnRoss
LinkedIn.com/in/EnjoyWrites

Joylynn's Favorite Resource
Act Like an Author, Think Like a Business: Ways to Achieve Financial Literary Success because of the results it has gotten for so many literary creatives.

Celebrate Your Success

Valerie J. Lewis Coleman

We are serious about helping you land paid speaking engagements, media attention, and book sales. Contact me at info@penofthewriter.com with the book you published using *Do It Right the First Time* as your resource. Your book will be
- Included in an eblast to my 30,000+ fans, friends, and followers.
- Listed on the Pen of the Writer (POWER) Wall of Fame.
- Entered for the Do It Right Bestseller where the top-selling title will be acknowledged each year.

Plus, I'll host a live panel-style interview to further magnify and monetize your message.

I want to serve more aspiring authors to achieve their publishing dreams and I need your help. Can you do me a favor by completing this list?
- Email me a testimonial about your experience with *Do It Right the First Time*. I'll share it on social media and my Google business page with a link to your site.
- Post your results on social media tagging me and the authors whose contributions helped you most. Create a viral thread using hashtags: #DoItRightTheFirstTime, #PenOfTheWriter, and #SelfPublishing.

- Write a review on Amazon at <u>https://amzn.to/3zeQ51j</u>. As Carolyn Howard-Johnson explained in *Do It Right the First Time: Conversations with Marketing Experts*, a bonus for writing reviews is that they hyperlink back to your author page.

Congrats in advance!

Your Bestseller Resources

"You were born to win, but to be a winner, you must plan to win, prepare to win, and expect to win."
—Zig Ziglar

Valerie J. Lewis Coleman

Publishing Resources

Talk with Val	https://penofthewriter.as.me
Affiliate Savings	PenOfTheWriter.com/powerful-affiliates ConstantContact, QuickBooks, Fiverr…
Amazon Author Page	Author.Amazon.com
Audiobook Production	ACX.com
Book Industry Study Group	BISG.org
Contract Publishing	QueenVPublishing.com
Copyright & Trademarks	Copyright.gov USPTO.gov
ISBN	Bowker.com MyIdentifiers.com
Legal Matters	Nakia Gray, Esq.'s Templates, Contracts, and Courses Bit.ly/LegalPOWER (case sensitive)
Pen of the Writer Academy	PenOfTheWriterAcademy.com
Print My Book	Bit.ly/POWERPrint (case sensitive)
Publishing Conferences	PathToPublishing.com/conference
Publishing Mentoring	CIPA.Podia.com Kindlepreneur.com

	PenOfTheWriter.com
	SelfPublishingAdvisor.com
Publishing Platforms	KDP.Amazon.com
	IngramSpark.com
Stock Images	BigStockPhoto.com
	IStockPhoto.com

Books on Publishing

Title	Author
Act Like an Author, Think Like a Business: Ways to Achieve Financial Literary Success	Joylynn Ross
Self-Publishing Made Easy: Purposeful Publishing https://bit.ly/3zwRiBx (case sensitive)	Valerie J. Lewis Coleman
Self-Publishing Manual	Dan Poynter

_____

_____

_____

_____

_____

_____

_____

_____

Marketing Resources

60 Minutes to Bestseller	Bit.ly/POWER60Mins (case sensitive)
Appointment Scheduler	https://acuity.jnqsge.net/zaa2RW (case sensitive)
CRM	ConstantContact.com HubSpot.com PipeDrive.com Save with promo code penofthewriter1851835
eCommerce	Paypal.com
File Sharing	DropBox.com WeTransfer.com
Headline Analyzer	AMInstitute.com/headline
Media	BlackGospelPromo.com BlackNews.com BlackPR.com Blavity.com DaytonWeeklyOnline.com HelpAReporter.com MadameNoire.com PRNewsWire.com RadioGuestList.com TheGrio.com TheRoot.com
Media Release	Email info@penofthewriter.com for samples of Pen of the Writer releases
Online Calendars	AALBC.com DaytonLit.com Writing.ShawGuide.com

Online Presence	Author.Amazon.com Bit.ly Google.com/alerts GoodReads.com GoDaddy.com Moz.com/domain-analysis#index TinyURL.com
Mastermind Networks	MightyNetworks.com TheMobMastermind.com
Merchandise	Affiliate-Program.Amazon.com Printful.com
Reviews	BookFunnel.com ReadersFavorite.com
Royalty-Free Music	EpidemicSound.com Pond5.com
Podcasts	Amazon.com/Live Anchor.fm ArtistFirst.com Bit.ly/POWERStreamYard (case sensitive) BlogTalkRadio.com Blubrry.com BuzzSprout.com GetAudioGram.com Headliner.app Kajabi.com Libsyn.com Spreaker.com
Promote	Animoto.com Canva.com RoboDial.org Txt180.com/sl/22m

	VistaPrint.com
	WheelOfNames.com
Promoters	LaShaundaHoffman.com
	SharHalliburton.com
Social Media Scheduling	Buffer.com
	HootSuite.com
	PostPlanner.com
	TailwindApp.com
Speaking Assistance	ToastMasters.org
Virtual Meetings & Training	FreeConferenceCall.com
	Kartra.com
	Zoom.com
Work for Hire	Fiverr.com
	TextBroker.com
	Upwork.com

Books on Marketing

Title	Author
Entrepreneur Secrets: The New Rules of Wealth Creation	Charlotte Howard
How to Do It Frugally	Carolyn Howard-Johnson
The Christian Writers Market Guide	Steve Laube
The Personal Touch: What You Really Need to Succeed in Today's Fast-Paced Business World	Terrie Williams
Sell Your Book Like Wildfire: The Writer's Guide to Marketing and Publicity	Rob Eager

Tradeshows and Conventions

American Library Association	ALA.org
Book Expo America	BookExpoAmerica.com
Christian Product Expo Show	CPEShow.com
National Religious Broadcasters Conventions	NRB.org
Podfest	PodFestExpo.com

Author Associations

Advanced Writers and Speakers Association	AWSA.com
American Christian Fiction Writers Association	ACFW.com
American Christian Writers	RegAForder.wordpress.com
Christian Authors Network	ChristianAuthorsNetwork.com
Christian Indie Publishing Association	ChristianPublishers.net
Evangelical Christian Publishers Association	ECPA.org
Military Writers Society of America	MWSADispatches.com
National Newspaper Publishers Association	NNPA.org
Nonfiction Authors Association	NonfictionAuthorsAssociation.com
Society of Children's Book Writers and Illustrators	SCBWI.org

Valerie J. Lewis Coleman

www.ingramcontent.com/pod-product-compliance
Lightning Source LLC
LaVergne TN
LVHW010223070526
838199LV00062B/4699